Alan Frank Keele is a professor of German language and literature at Brigham Young University. He received a B.A. degree in German and History from Brigham Young University and earned his Ph.D. degree at Princeton University under Theodore Ziolkowski. He has written two other books on postwar German literature, one on the author Paul Schallück and one about themes in postwar German literature. He has also written about topics as varied as the resistance movement to Hitler and the notion of the pre-existence of the human soul as reflected in the arts. Keele is currently working with German author Walter Kempowski, from whose works he has prepared a computerized word-index as an aid in interpretation.

Understanding
GÜNTER GRASS

UNDERSTANDING CONTEMPORARY EUROPEAN and LATIN AMERICAN LITERATURE

JAMES HARDIN, *SERIES EDITOR*

UNDERSTANDING

GÜNTER
GRASS

ALAN FRANK KEELE

UNIVERSITY OF SOUTH CAROLINA PRESS

Published in Columbia, South Carolina, by the
University of South Carolina Press

LIBRARY OF CONGRESS
Library of Congress Cataloging-in-Publication Data

Keele, Alan Frank.
   Understanding Günter Grass / Alan Frank Keele.
      p. cm.—(Understanding contemporary European and Latin
American literature)
   Bibliography: p.
   Includes index.
   ISBN 0-87249-546-9.   ISBN 0-87249-547-7 (pbk.)
   1. Grass, Günter, 1927–   —Criticism and interpretation.
I. Title.   II. Series.
PT2613.R338Z687   1988
833′.914—dc19   87–30061
                                                                        CIP

CONTENTS

UNDERSTANDING CONTEMPORARY EUROPEAN AND Latin American Literature has been planned as a series of guides for students and nonacademic readers. Like its companion series, *Understanding Contemporary American Literature,* the aim of the books is to provide a brief introduction to the life and writings of prominent contemporary authors and to explicate their most important works.

Contemporary literature makes special demands, and this is particularly true of foreign literature, in which the reader must contend not only with unfamiliar, often arcane artistic conventions and philosophical concepts, but also with the handicap of reading the literature in translation. It is a truism that the nuances of one language can be rendered in another only imperfectly (and this problem is especially difficult in fiction), but the fact that the works of European and Latin American writers are situated in a historical and cultural setting quite different from our own can be as great a hindrance to the understanding of these works as the linguistic barrier. For this reason, the *UCELL* series will emphasize the sociological and historical background of the writers treated. The peculiar philosophical and cultural traditions of a given culture may be particularly important for an understanding of certain authors, and these will be taken up in the introductory chapter and also in the discussion of those works to which this information is relevant. Beyond this, the books will treat the specifically literary aspects of the author under discussion and attempt to explain the complexities of contemporary literature lucidly. The books are conceived as introductions to the authors covered, not as comprehensive analyses. They do not provide summaries of plot, as they are meant to be used in conjunction with the books they treat, not as a substitute for the study of the original works.

It is our hope that the *UCELL* series will help to increase our understanding of the European and Latin American cultures and will serve to make the path to the literature of those cultures more accessible.

J.H.

PREFACE

THE OEUVRE OF GÜNTER GRASS IS LARGE AND COMPLEX. His published belles lettres alone run well over 5,000 pages and his expository writings account for thousands more. It is also important to note that his works are closely linked to the course of the author's eventful life. This means that any adequate treatment of Günter Grass must go beyond a brief career summary to include some detailed biographical information.

In the interest of clarity and economy I have chosen to discuss Grass's life and his major works of prose fiction in an essentially chronological delineation. Because of its seminal importance as a model for all the rest, the first of these, *Die Blechtrommel* (*The Tin Drum*), is analyzed in somewhat more detail. Other works—essays, poems, plays, ballet librettos—even when they are not all individually or exhaustively explicated, are illuminated by the discussion of both the period in which they were created and that of the major prose works with which they are so closely linked.

This strategy intentionally sidesteps the relatively early plays and related poems, some of the most difficult of Grass's works. These are treated last, allowing all the understanding gained from the prose works and from Grass's entire career to be focused upon them.

In a final brief excursus a representative example of Grass's expository writing is analyzed and linked to the belles lettres. The reader should then have the confidence to approach and begin to understand the works of Günter Grass, of whatever genre, including those not specifically treated in this book.

Although the English translations of the original German are my own, I have always gratefully consulted and have often borrowed from the published translations by Ralph Manheim and Michael Hamburger, among others.

A.F.K.

Book titles cited in the text have been abbreviated as shown below. Page numbers following these abbreviations refer to the respective original (hardback) German edition, to the collected plays (Ts), or to the original (paperback) 1971 edition of the collected poems (GG).

AL = *Aufsätze zur Literatur*
AT = *Aus dem Tagebuch einer Schnecke*
BS = *Der Bürger und seine Stimme*
Bt = *Die Blechtrommel*
DB = *Der Butt*
DR = *Die Rättin*
GG = *Gesammelte Gedichte*
Hj = *Hundejahre*
Kg = *Kopfgeburten oder Die Deutschen sterben aus*
KM = *Katz und Maus*
Me = *Mariazuehren*
öb = *örtlich betäubt*
Ts = *Theaterspiele*
TT = *Das Treffen in Telgte*
ÜS = *Über das Selbstverständliche*
ZS = *Zeichnen und Schreiben*

Understanding
GÜNTER GRASS

INTRODUCTION

GÜNTER GRASS IS MORE THAN A WRITER; HE IS A PHE-
nomenon. Recognized in Germany by friend and foe
alike as a formidable artistic, moral, and political
force, abroad he is viewed almost as a personification
of Germany and of postwar German literature. Yet
Grass has never pandered to his own popularity—far
from it. What he writes, says, and does is just as
likely to strike an open nerve as a responsive chord.
His fame and his infamy (in his case hardly too
strong a word) are both aftereffects of the single-
minded pursuit of his mission: to make of Germany's
Nazi experience a moral yardstick, to reduce it to a
kind of ethical absolute zero against which to measure all other tendencies, past, present, or future.

Though he might under other circumstances have
become a historian, Grass is an artist, not a scholar.
For him art is a more useful vehicle for capturing
fleeting phenomena, for objectifying and assembling
even wildly disparate things in the same medium, on
the same plane, in the same scale, where they can be
scrutinized and compared. Those, of course, who follow the aesthetic logic of his demonstrations might
think them elegant; those who do not might call
them far-fetched, absurd, pornographic, or even blas-
phemous.

In his controversial quest for truth Grass has not
been satisfied with any single mode of artistic inquiry: though he began as a sculptor, he has become

3

a many-faceted artist, a writer of lyric poetry, drama, narrative prose, ballet librettos, and political tracts; a sculptor, painter, graphic designer, etcher; and, most recently, an aspiring cinematographer. Many of his ideas seem to have been worked out across various genres in his repertory and reduced to a system of remarkably durable symbols that have continued to inform his oeuvre over a period of more than three decades.

For Günter Grass no symbols are more durable than those crafted from his immediate life and experience. In more than the usual ways Grass and his unique perspectives are a direct result of the place and timing of his birth. Danzig, now Gdansk in Poland, was in 1927 a German-speaking island surrounded by the Polish Corridor to the Baltic Sea. It was a free city created by the victorious Allies after World War I. When the Nazis came to power in Germany in 1933, they began to organize in Danzig as well. Bringing Danzig "home to the Reich" became one of their rallying cries. In the early morning hours of September 1, 1939, the first shots of World War II were fired in Danzig, in the attack on the Polish Post Office.

Grass has said that in Danzig the Nazis' rise to power occurred slowly, almost as a microcosmic model, so that one could take notes. And take notes he did. From his perspective as a child, the impressionable and gifted boy simultaneously absorbed the minute details of life in a petit-bourgeois family in the Labesweg, a street in the Danzig suburb of Langfuhr, and the making of global war and holocaust. Small wonder then, that Grass's artistic search for the

4

causes of evil still concentrates on minutiae: on subtleties of language, of prejudice and political accommodation, of misplaced sexual and religious fervor.

His mother was descended from Kashubians, a Slavic people distinct from the Poles. Most members of her family were farmers who lived near the village of Karthaus, southwest of Danzig. One of the uncles, Franz, worked at the Polish Post Office. Grass's father's side of the family was German. His grandfather owned a moderately large cabinetmaking shop, and Grass's parents kept a small neighborhood grocery store. These environments and many others, like those of the schools and churches Grass attended, become important artistic settings, microcosmic mises-en-scènes for his aesthetic reconstructions of the genesis of evil.

His view of this genesis is that of an insider: he does not exempt himself from guilt. Only his youth prevented Grass from being more responsible for Nazi atrocities. If he had been born earlier, he says, he would have been just as zealous as any other Nazi. As it was, even as a child he was very much involved. At ten he was a member of the *Jungvolk*, the "cubs" of the Nazi Party. At fourteen he became a Hitler Youth, at fifteen a volunteer helper at an antiaircraft battery, and at seventeen he was a tank gunner. Wounded in a battle near Cottbus in late April of 1945, he was taken to a field hospital in Marienbad, Czechoslovakia. There he was captured by the advancing American forces. While in an American prisoner-of-war camp in Bavaria, he was taken as a reeducation measure to visit the concentration camp at Dachau, where for the first time, he says, he began earnestly to question the validity of the Nazi point of view.

After he was released from the POW camp, Grass worked on a farm and then spent a year as a laborer in a potash mine. At the mine his political reeducation continued. Grass reports that whenever the electrical power failed, as it often did in those years, the miners would gather around in the light of their carbide lamps, 3,000 feet underground, and engage in political discussions. He recalls that he began to see how the Nazis and the Communists shared what he calls the same dusty ideology and how they quickly banded together to oppose the Social Democrats.

The Social Democrats for their part, he says, were more practical: they had long since disposed of any ideological baggage like the thousand-year Reich or World Revolution (ÜS 72f). In the spring of 1947 Grass went to nearby Hannover to hear a speech by the Social Democratic politician Kurt Schumacher, whose arguments further convinced Grass of the superiority of the Social Democratic position.

In 1947 Grass moved to Düsseldorf to study sculpting at the Art Academy. Because of a shortage of coal, however, the academy was temporarily closed, so one of the professors made the practical suggestion that Grass become an apprentice stonemason, at least for the time being. Later he entered the academy and studied sculpture under Sepp Mages and graphics under Otto Pankok. In the evenings he played in the rhythm section of a jazz band organized by a fellow art student, Horst Geldmacher. Many of these details—the academy, the band and the restaurants it played in, as well as twists on the names

6

of his teachers and friends (for instance, Geldmacher, "money maker," becoming Münzer, "minter," or Pankok, "pancake," becoming Kuchen, "cake")—recur in Grass's later works.

After a trip through Italy in 1951 and a hitch-hiking tour of France in 1952, Grass moved to Berlin to study metal sculpting under Karl Hartung. In 1954 he married the Swiss dancer Anna Schwarz, through whom he became interested in dance and because of whom he began to write ballets.

Grass's earliest efforts at writing had begun when, as a thirteen-year-old, he entered a "novel" entitled "Die Kaschuben" (The Kashubians) in a writing contest sponsored by a Nazi school magazine. During his art studies after the war he began to write again. In 1955 he was awarded the third prize in a poetry contest sponsored by South German Radio.

Walter Höllerer, editor of the literary magazine *Akzente*, took an interest in Grass and published some of his poems, short plays, and essays. His first book, a volume of poetry entitled *Die Vorzüge der Windhühner* (The Advantages of Wind Chickens) appeared in 1956. His early plays "Hochwasser" ("Flood") and "Onkel, Onkel" ("Mister, Mister"), as well as his ballet "Stoffreste" (Cloth Remnants), had their premieres, some arranged for by Walter Höllerer, in small experimental theaters around Germany.

In 1955, at its Berlin meeting, he had read some of his works before the *Gruppe 47* (Group 47), an informal but extremely influential association of politically active publicists with literary ambitions organized in 1947 by Hans Werner Richter. Grass was to become one of this group's most famous and most loyal members. Even at this first meeting with the Group 47 in 1955 Grass's talent was recognized, and he received encouragement from at least one older member, Paul Schallück, to try his hand at a novel.

The next year, 1956, he and Anna moved to Paris, she to study dance and he to work in earnest on the novel eventually entitled *The Tin Drum*. In 1958 Höllerer helped arrange for Grass to return to Gdansk to do research at the site of the attack on the Polish Post Office and on other details of *The Tin Drum*, now nearing completion. The trip was partially financed by the 5,000 Mark prize of the Group 47 that he won by reading in manuscript the beginning section of the novel. When it appeared in print the next year, 1959, it was an "event" of the first magnitude.

Critical reception of *The Tin Drum* was sharply polarized: for each of the numerous literary prizes it was awarded, the book evoked countless howls of indignation as well as legal actions alleging pornography and blasphemy. A characteristic case was that of the city of Bremen. Its prestigious literary prize was originally awarded to Grass by the judges but blocked in an unusual action by the Social Democratic Municipal Senate, by no means a reactionary body, out of concern that the city might be perceived as having given official sanction to some kind of literary anarchist or pornographer.

The polarity of its reception may be partly explained on the basis of the narrative strategy of the novel itself. In a cursory or unsophisticated reading *The Tin Drum* might appear to consist merely of the scurrilous, self-indulgent rantings of a misbegotten gnome, an inmate of an institution for the criminally insane, one Oskar Matzerath. To make matters worse, Grass seems to show the greatest sympathy toward this character, and it is obvious even to those who know Grass only vaguely that the novel is fundamentally autobiographical: Oskar lives in Danzig, in the Labesweg, where his parents own a neighborhood grocery store. After the war he moves to Düsseldorf, where he works as a stonemason, a jazz drummer, and at the Art Academy.

What such a reading of the novel might fail to reveal is that these two levels, the biographical narrative of Oskar Matzerath and the closely related life of Günter Grass, are themselves subordinate to the intent of the work: to investigate the rise of dictatorship, war, and holocaust. The life history of Oskar Matzerath is merely an adumbration, a visible, microcosmic scratching of an artistic seismograph needle. It records not only the violent global upheavals of world history in the twentieth century but also the subtle foreshocks and aftershocks as well. Each beat of the sticks on Oskar's mnemonic drum, each jiggle of Oskar's pen recorded on the pages of *The Tin Drum,* is a reaction to ever-larger forces in ever-widening spheres of his family, his neighborhood, all of Danzig, Germany, and the world.

But Oskar does not simply record these forces. He is also a victim of them a participant in them. He is an artist with no choice but to make a record of his evil times. He is a blue-eyed "drummer" with a messiah complex because that also describes Adolf Hitler, a man possessed of striking blue eyes, who with his tub-thumping rhetoric was known as the drummer—a savior figure called by God to lead Germany into the (millennial) thousand-year Reich.

Oskar's voice breaks glass because he lives in an age of broken glass like that of the "Crystal Night" in November 1938, when Jewish shops were attacked and synagogues burned. He is a liar and murderer because he mirrors the lying and murderous time and place in which he lives. He becomes a Jesus to a gang of vandals because he lives in a society of violent true believers seeking a *Führer*. He is a dwarf because he lives in an age of moral dwarves. He grows into a misshapen hunchback in 1945 because it is his fate to reflect the distorted boundaries and values of postwar Germany and of the postwar world.

In the last analysis *The Tin Drum* is not the story of an obscene dwarf, based on the autobiography of a vulgar author. The linkage is the other way around. The novel is the story of historical obscenity in our century, told by the very incarnation of the *Zeitgeist*, whose curriculum vitae corresponds to the author's only to the extent that the author himself feels that he, too, is a man produced by and typical of his age.

CHAPTER ONE

The Tin Drum
(Die Blechtrommel)

THE KEY TO UNDERSTANDING *THE TIN DRUM* LIES IN understanding the mind of its remarkable first-person narrator, Oskar Matzerath, that brilliantly conceived fictional eyewitness and personification of the Third Reich, its prehistory, and its aftermath. It is certainly not a normal mind. Oskar confesses in the very first words of his history that he is a mental patient. He is, as we eventually learn, accused of murder. His first sentence, with its claim that his blue eyes make him inscrutable to his brown-eyed male nurse Bruno, is itself a disjointed non sequitur, exuding both paranoid schizophrenia and delusions of Nordic supremacy. The verb *vorlügen* (to tell lies) in the fourth sentence reveals that his narrative, at first told orally to Bruno and then recorded on "innocent" white paper, is full of prevarication. Yet he is motivated by his guilt to include so much self-incriminating truth that he says he must write his confessions without the knowledge of his lawyer or of his friend Klepp, who is helping to have him freed. Both of them would surely consider it dangerous to his case to entrust Oskar with blank paper.

Book 1: The Prewar Years

Oskar begins the story proper with an account of his mother's conception in the fall of 1899. The grippingly unconventional style of the narrative is only one of the qualities attributable to and made possible by Oskar's abnormality. His infantile fixation on female genitalia and on the womb is another, as is his related desire to return to his origins under the skirts of his grandmother, whom he identifies—in part olfactorily—with the Great Earth Mother.[1] Other such megalomanic attempts to lend to his own life a higher, mythical significance include his linking of a rather unbelievable account of a bizarre and physically impossible coitus in a potato field with certain references to the immaculate conception of St. Anne and of the Virgin. Here she follows her Joseph, if not to Egypt, at least to Danzig (Bt 22).

But for the reader willing to decode this narrative, there is much method in Oskar's madness. His story *is* more universal in significance than that of a normal individual, and it is fraught with cosmic omens, as Oskar reveals when he describes his mother's birth in 1900: "At the end of July of the year zero zero—it was just being decided to double the building program for the Imperial Battle Fleet—Mama saw the light of day under the zodiacal sign of Leo" (Bt 22).

Read not merely as a far-fetched and inappropriate non sequitur but as a link to history, this parenthetical interjection about the Imperial Fleet, like the one a few lines before about the impending Boer

12

War, hints that the birth of Oskar's mother is a symbol for the birth of an epoch, a century in which preparations are being made for global war. Oskar then proceeds to cast his mother's cryptic horoscope, which involves confused marital relationships, fish, eels, illness, a celebration of annihilation, and a dwelling in the deadly house. This accurately presages not only his mother's unhappy *ménage à trois* with her German husband, Alfred Matzerath, and her Polish cousin, Jan Bronski—as well as her untimely death by self-inflicted fish and eel poisoning—but, by a system of ever-widening symbolic circles, the future of Danzig, Germany, and the world.

There are other unsettling omens in Oskar's—and our epoch's—lineage: his grandmother's brother, Vinzent Bronski, is a gentle but unhinged visionary to whom the Black Madonna of Czestochowa had revealed her wish to be the Queen of Poland. (Such confusion of religious mysticism with political reality is one of Günter Grass's most persistent concerns.) Vinzent's misshapen son Jan, Oskar's presumptive father, is a full cousin of Oskar's mother, thus making Oskar a double heir to Vinzent's congenital dementia and to his role as a visionary as well as to Jan's blue eyes.

We are also reminded by Jan's blue eyes, here specifically compared to those of Adolf Hitler (Bt 307), that Hitler came from similarly incestuous ancestry. Consulting a pedigree chart of the inbred Hitler clan[2] further serves to confirm our impression that Oskar is more than a mere individual. He is a pathological personification of his times.

Oskar's maternal grandfather, Joseph Koljaiczek,

is also a fanatic, an incendiary out of nationalistic fervor. In this case too Oskar informs us that the Virgin Mary, wearing the Crown of Poland, is said to appear on the roofs of sawmills set on fire by his grandfather. This political firebug goes into hiding, takes on the identity of one Joseph Wranka, and joins a volunteer fire department whose captain is a certain Pastor Hecht. When questions arise about Koljaiczek's true identity, Hecht, at least as reported by the ever mythopoetic and mythomaniac narrator Oskar, speaks to his congregation in parables about the heavenly fireman and the hellish firebug.

Oskar extends the mythic and the global dimensions of the symbol by suggesting alternate possibilities following Joseph's probable death under a raft of logs. Like the narrator of Grass's next work, *Cat and Mouse*, who toys with the mythic idea of a miraculous resurrection from a watery grave, Oskar imagines his grandfather living in Buffalo, USA as a kind of Joseph the Provider of incendiary materials. He is a wealthy stockholder in match factories, a dealer in lumber products, and, ironically, a founder of fire insurance companies. Perhaps Oskar, the heir to all this politico-religious pyromania, could join his grandsire in America, he imagines, after his impending release from the asylum.

With another of his unexpected interjections, that ubiquitous technique juxtaposing events from Oskar's private life with those of a universal, historical nature, Oskar subtly finishes the story of his grandfather. He drums Koljaiczek's departure for America in march rhythms symbolizing the beginning of World War I. Thus he links the private band of mourners for Koljaiczek with those who will mourn for the victims of the impending war.

At the end of the war Danzig is made a free city under the League of Nations—an act which was to be the cause of new wars, Oskar says. One of his private symbols for the growing tension between Germans and Poles in Danzig is the marriage of Oskar's mother to the German Matzerath, a Rhinelander who had been slightly wounded in the war and sent to a hospital in Danzig. As an act of political protest, Jan Bronski has himself transferred to the Polish Post Office, and Oskar's grandmother moves back across the Polish border to live with her brother Vinzent on the farm.

Oskar's account of his own birth is couched in especially mythic terms. The biblical text "Let there be light, and there was light" is invoked in reference to the light bulbs in the bedroom. Oskar also claims to have been a clairaudient infant, fully omniscient from birth. In order to disguise his incredible precociousness at birth, he claims he pretended—outwardly only—to be a crying, blue-red newborn like any other. Portentously, evoking the sound of approaching shellfire in the years to come, a thunderstorm is heard and seen in the distance. It makes the furniture in the room appear to move just as later shellfire will actually move it.

As befitting his fixation on his own role as a Jesus figure, on his mother's as a fallen virgin, and on his future involvement with a girl named Maria, Oskar tells us that he was born under the sign of Virgo, the Virgin. Libra was in the ascendancy, Oskar says, which made him sensitive and tempted him to exaggerations. Neptune anchors him between miracles and deception, and Saturn casts doubt on his origins.

His mother states that he should have a tin drum when he turns three. That, together with the drumming of a moth on the light bulbs and the rhythm of the distant thunder imprint upon Oskar the indelible desire to be a drummer, he recounts. This momentarily overrides even his desire to return to the womb.

At his side in the asylum Oskar has an old photo album which, together with his drum, is the wellspring of his memories of the past. With a compass, a triangle, and a ruler he seeks, and believes he finds, mathematical and cosmic references on a photo showing the "trinity" of his mother and his two presumptive fathers. On the first photo of himself as a three-year-old with his new tin drum, Oskar believes he sees reflected in each of his blue eyes the will to power, the will to remain a three-year-old, yet thrice as intelligent as any adult. At three Oskar is fully developed internally and externally. Only his phallus later grows, he implies, and attains "messianic greatness" (Bt 67).

Oskar maintains that he staged a fall down the cellar steps in order to give the adults a logical medical reason for his interrupted growth. In view of his penchant for prevarication, however, leaving aside for a moment his very high potential for congenital abnormality, it seems more likely that the fall on his head was the cause of his retardation. (At the end of World War II, at Alfred Matzerath's burial when Oskar begins to grow a bit and develop a hunchback, we will see that he again tries to portray his growth as an act of will. A bit later he confesses, however, to having been hit on the head by a stone, a blow which symbolically parallels the invasion of Germany and the overthrow of fascism.) In any event, for the time being, the fictional effect is largely the same: Oskar remains a child, able, almost unnoticed, to observe society in its most intimate, and most evil, affairs.

In a new development coinciding with his fall, Oskar suddenly finds he is able to shatter glass with his voice, something which adds substantially to the symbolic significance of this episode. Oskar's fall, for which Alfred Matzerath is repeatedly blamed—he had left the "*Fall*tür" (trap door) to the cellar open— functions as a subtle, symbolic foretoken of the fall of democratic order. Oskar's retarded growth functions as a symbol of the end to the process of political maturation under the Weimar Republic. (Matzerath's early entry into the Nazi Party further underscores his guilt—and the political symbolism—in the matter. So does his death during the Soviet invasion of the last days of the war when he quite literally chokes to death on his Nazi Party pin.)

Oskar uses his ability to shatter glass to tempt others, including Jan, to incur guilt and "fall" by stealing from shop windows. (The evil principle, he says, made him break out a piece of glass like a "*Fall*tür" allowing Jan to steal a ruby collar for Oskar's mother [Bt 157].) This becomes more and more clearly a foreshadowing of that vandalism, thievery, and anti-Semitism which had become an officially sanctioned instrument of state policy by the Crystal Night of November 9–10, 1938—its very name refers

17

to the broken glass from Jewish shop windows. The Crystal Night itself then is a foreshadowing of the really great age of broken glass in the war to follow. "Hence my work was a destructive one," Oskar summarizes (Bt 147), albeit in reference to another of his activities: the disruption of political rallies of all kinds, including Nazi rallies, in parallel to actual disruptions of the orderly democratic process by beer-hall thugs of various political stripes.

At Oskar's first demonstration of his glass-breaking powers, when he destroys the crystal of the grandfather clock, he claims that Jan Bronski moved his lips in a silent prayer, perhaps in the *Miserere nobis*. Oskar relates this in order to hint that Jan recognized Oskar's messianic greatness. But the prayer "Have mercy on us" may also inadvertently suggest that this small act of destruction is a portent of impending global catastrophe.

As time passes, Oskar witnesses more and more hatred and violence, at first in small but significant events such as the beating suffered by little Stephan Bronski, Jan's son, in Fräulein Kauer's kindergarten at the hands of a child with the Germanic name Lothar, who hisses "Polack" between blows. "He can't help it that he's a little Pole," Fräulein Kauer sweetly explains, reinforcing the prejudice if not the epithet (Bt 85).

Oskar himself hears the neighborhood children, Axel Mischke, Nuchi Eyke, and the rest, singing the nursery rhyme "Ist die Schwarze Köchin da? Jajaja!" (Where's the Black Cook, is she here? Yes, she's here!). Then he is forced by them to eat some of their frog, urine, and brick soup, which Oskar refers to as an *Eintopfgericht* (Bt 113), that one-dish meal mandated by the Nazis to save food and money for the war effort.

Later, as adolescents, they force him to play doctor and swallow spoonfuls of a mysterious serum which is quite probably semen. Shortly thereafter Oskar sees them in uniforms participating now in organized, grown-up intimidation and violence, ending ultimately in the war.

Oskar's friend Herbert Truczinski perishes when he chops a double-bitted ax into Niobe, the legendary man- and boy-killing wooden figurehead in the maritime museum, and then runs the ax into his own chest when he attempts to rape her. Niobe is banned to a storeroom in the cellar after she causes Herbert's death, but from this cellar room the malaise finds its way through the sewers into the gas pipes and is fed to all the unsuspecting households.

Oskar's visionary mind concatenates the evil implied in the cooking of the children's urine *Eintopf*, in the Black Cook, and in the fatal essence of Niobe. Finally, Oskar's concatenations of this miasmal essence of evil lead him to the Heavenly Gasman, without whom the people cannot cook: "An entire gullible people believed in Santa Claus," Oskar writes of the events following the Crystal Night before Christmas, 1938, "but Santa Claus was in reality the Gasman" (Bt 244).

If Santa Claus brings fruits and nuts, more specifically almonds, this Heavenly Gasman brings potassium cyanide, which happens to smell like almonds. (Grass later makes this connection in more detail in *From the Diary of a Snail*, 1972.) Instead of bringing

Christmas sausages or mincemeat *to* humanity, this Gasman makes sausage or mincemeat *of* humanity. As soon as his true believers had declared faith in him to be the state religion, the Heavenly Gasman would not only unleash the great war and the Holocaust, but he would return in the future, Oskar writes—his fear made palpable by his frenzied style—with more frightening things in his bag.

A starkly ironic light is shed on the nature of this evil by the story of the trumpet-playing, alcoholic Meyn, who gives up liquor—thus losing his ability to play beautifully, Oskar says—to join the mounted storm troopers of the SA, the brown-shirted *Sturmabteilung*. In his new, sober state, and saddened by the death of his neighbor and classmate Herbert at the maritime museum, Meyn hits his four smelly tomcats with a poker and throws them in a trash can. When the tenderhearted watchmaker Laubschad sees the lid of the can moving, he removes the cats and tries unsuccessfully to save their lives.

As a member of the Nazi Party animal protection league, Laubschad files a complaint against Meyn. Because his deed was injurious to the image of the Party, Meyn is dishonorably ejected from the storm troopers and goes back to drink. In due course he ends as an "asocial element" in a concentration camp, even though he had performed with exceptional bravery during the Crystal Night. He had helped in burning down one of the Danzig synagogues—Matzerath warms his hands and his feelings over the blaze of yet another—and smashing several Jewish shops, albeit not the toy store where Oskar gets his tin drums. There, other sober SA men in the same brown shirts had done their honorable, humane work: smashing in windows, defecating on the merchandise, and so frightening the owner, Sigismund Markus, that he commits suicide.

In the meantime Oskar has been baptized. Satan does not depart from him, we read, but whispers "Did you see the church windows, Oskar? They're all glass, all glass!" (Bt 162). His messiah complex deepens when he sees that he closely resembles the statue of Jesus on the lap of the Madonna. He returns to the church to teach Jesus to play his drum. For the moment he is disappointed when such a miracle does not occur, though it will later, during the war, when Oskar becomes a "Jesus" to his following of juvenile delinquents known as the Duster Gang.

Oskar also goes to school, at least for part of the first day. He is dismissed after his screams break the classroom windows and the teacher's glasses. He claims he learned to read with Gretchen Scheffler, the wife of the neighborhood baker. She owns one book about Rasputin and another by Goethe, pages from both of which Oskar gradually steals and shuffles together into a kind of reader. Rasputin and Goethe, like Beethoven and Hitler, whose pictures stare at each other across the Matzerath's sitting room, represent the two poles of Oskar's and of the European soul: genius and lunatic. The balance—reflected by Oskar's preference and the prized position over the piano, respectively—is tilting rapidly, even among the ladies of proper bourgeois society, toward the lunatics. Oskar's mother and Gretchen Scheffler become so aroused by the accounts of Rasputin's orgies that they engage in their own orgies of mutual masturbation. Political implications are never far beneath the surface: Oskar's reference to the murder of Rasputin at the hands of military officers echoes the officers' plot of July 20, 1944, against Hitler, he says.

Analogous political implications of this rising irrational and immoral tide emanate from the continuing incestuous adultery of Oskar's mother and Jan Bronski. Reading carefully between Oskar's intentionally enigmatic lines reveals that when she becomes pregnant she fears giving birth to another monstrosity such as Oskar. So she attempts to abort the fetus by stuffing herself with fish and eels (food that makes her deathly sick since she witnessed on Good Friday an old man catching eels in a horse's head), eventually to die of food poisoning and hepatitis.

Her death prompts Oskar to indulge in eucharistic/ necrophagous speculations: in lieu of the false Jesus in the church who was unable to perform a miracle on his drum, it is Oskar's mother who descends to the grave, taking her three-month old fetus and bits of eel with her. This eel had possibly fed on the corpses of sailors after the battle of Skagerrak, the mythomaniac Oskar speculates, once more linking her death to the war (in *Cat and Mouse* torpedoes are also referred to by the slang term "eel"). Or it had possibly fed on the corpse of her father, Joseph Koljaiczek, who disappeared under the raft of logs: "Eel to eel," Oskar mystically intones (Bt 195).

Her demise, accurately "forecast" by her horoscope—one must not forget that Oskar is creating his book well after the fact—is itself a symbolic "fore-

cast" of the demise of Danzig and Germany. This is
further demonstrated by a game of skat, the three-
handed card game which had once been the ideal
symbol of and rationale for the *ménage à trois*. After
her death, the German Nazi cell leader Alfred Matzerath and the Polish Post Office employee Jan
Bronski meet at midnight to play symbolic hands of
skat: "Poland has just lost a Grand Slam," Oskar reports; "the Free City of Danzig has just won a blockbuster diamond full house for the Greater German
Reich" (Bt 257).

Book 2: The War Years

Book 1 closes with Oskar's terror-stricken visions
of the advent of the Heavenly Gasman, with the
account of the Crystal Night, and the political perversion of the Pauline ideals faith, hope, and charity.
The skat game at the beginning of Book 2, then,
with its portentous military language, leads directly
to the advent of the first open hostilities of World
War II, commencing at 4:45 on the morning of
September 1, 1939, with the attack on the Polish
Post Office. Oscar, as *Zeitgeist*, manages to be on
hand for this momentous occasion, as he will be as
well in June 1944, during the Allied landings in Normandy.

Deprived of his mother's care and his supply of
new drums from Sigismund Markus, as the ominous
chapter title "Scrap Metal" implies, by the evening of
the last day of August 1939 Oskar has reduced his

old drum to a battered wreck, a preview of the universal wreckage soon to follow. He finds Jan Bronski, who takes him through the German barricades to the Polish Post Office in order, Oskar thinks, to have the janitor Kobyella repair his drum. From the fact that Jan is sweating profusely and from the comments made by his co-workers when he arrives at the Post Office, however, we infer that Jan had decided to stay away from his duty to defend the Post Office until he met, in Oskar, the personification of his fate, a reminder of the skat games, of his German competitor Alfred Matzerath, and of his patriotic duty to Poland.

Oskar falls asleep in a cart full of mail, which could have symbolized the world, he says, thereby underscoring the Post Office's role as a microcosmic point of departure for global conflict. Early the next morning he is awakened by the sound of gunfire, which could just as well have been a late-summer thunderstorm like the one at his birth. The German heavy machine guns certainly have the same effect on the Post Office windows as his voice, he observes. If he had used his voice he could have eliminated all the glass in the buildings across the street, he claims. But this would have been an anachronism, giving premature rise to the idea of *Wunderwaffen* (miracle weapons) in which Hitler and his followers were to put so much stock later in the war.

Oskar finds Kobyella and Jan in the nursery of the flat belonging to Postal Secretary Naczalnik, whose family has been evacuated. The explosion of a shell knocks down a new tin drum from a high shelf for

Oskar and mortally wounds Kobyella, whom Jan and Oskar drag into the safety of a windowless mail room. There the three of them continue the symbolic game of skat—Oskar drops his infantile disguise and plays like an adult—this time representing Poland and its allies England and France. Though they do not rush to Poland's aid, they will, as the course of the oracular game convinces Oskar, eventually succeed. The defense of the Polish Post Office will not have been in vain.

But before this ultimate victory, as the fall of the house of cards built by Jan suggests to him—German soldiers bursting into the room cause it to fall—Oskar fears that a day would have to come when "all the things stuck together which we call architecture . . . would give up their cohesiveness" (Bt 301).

Eventually Oskar corrects his first account of Jan's arrest. Oskar's pen may have been exaggerating, he admits, if not actually lying. In the corrected account he calls his performance a "Judas act" (Bt 300)—lending mythical meaning to his previous statement "I kissed him portentously" (Bt 295). According to this statement Oskar begins to cry and point accusingly at Jan. The fatherly Germans then take Jan for an inhumane, barbaric Polish kidnapper intending to use an innocent child as a shield against bullets. As if to complete the grotesque passion, the outraged soldiers kick Jan "ins Kreuz" (in the back, literally: the cross).

At bottom, Oskar's pretended ignorance and innocence of his father's death is a symbol, he says, for something which came into fashion about this time and behind which many are still hiding today: a pretended ignorance and innocence about the crimes of the Third Reich.

After the fall of the Polish Post Office and Oskar's discovery, with the aid of the demented graveyard spook Schugger Leo, that Jan Bronski has been shot and buried at the small cemetery at Saspe—Leo finds a spent cartridge shell and a skat card there which Oskar gives his grandmother—one might expect Oskar's narrative to continue with a detailed account of the further course of the war. But now we hear only through the fittingly distant medium of the radio about the progress of the distant hostilities. The war makes only an occasional parenthetical protrusion into the foreground in the form of special bulletins. Instead, equating his own messianic phallus with Hitler's weapons of war, Oskar gives an account of his own sexual exploits, thereby making his failed erotic conquests into a series of symbols for Germany's unsuccessful military ventures.

His first failed conquest is Maria, Herbert Truczinski's younger sister, whom the widower Matzerath engages to work in his grocery store. Oskar would have his readers believe that with the help of ordinary fizz powder (which he places in Maria's hand one day at the beach, adding his saliva to create a prickling, tingling sensation, thus causing her to be sexually aroused) he eventually impregnates her, albeit as she sleeps, he admits. And though Oskar subsequently refers to himself as the father of her son, Kurt, it is clear that he causes her pregnancy only in the sense that he interrupts a *coitus interruptus* between Maria and Matzerath by jumping onto Matzerath's back at the moment of ejaculation, thus preventing Matzerath's withdrawal.

Shortly thereafter the radio interrupts its broadcast of Strauss waltzes to report that German U-boats had torpedoed so-and-so-many British ships. With the conventional slang phrase "in den Grund bohren" (literally: to drill into the bottom), Grass makes another subtle connection between the sexual and the military (Bt 355), a device used even more obviously later on in *Cat and Mouse.*

In the case of Oskar it is clear that his messianic phallicism, his claim of potency and procreative success (he aims to found a dynasty of drummers capable of procreation, he says) all starkly contrasting with his actual "bleierne Ohnmacht" (Bt 357; in this context: leaden *impotence*), forms a perfect symbol for Germany's delusions of a global military prowess based on hot lead.

This becomes even more clear from the four chapters in the exact middle of Book 2 that document the major turning points of the war. The first two, entitled "Bearing His Impotence to Mrs. Greff" and "Seventy-five Kilos," graphically link an account of the problems of the German armies stuck in the mud on the Eastern Front to Oskar's sordid masturbatory activities with the obese Frau Greff (to whom Oskar turns after Matzerath marries Maria), the neglected wife of a homosexual greengrocer and former boy scout leader: "Vyazma and Bryansk; then the mud period set in. Oskar, too, began to wallow energetically in the mud in the middle of October 1941 . . . similar to how tanks and trucks bogged down just outside of Moscow, I bogged down" (Bt 376).

The greengrocer is aware of these unnatural sexual activities, but as the German Sixth Army "conquers" Stalingrad on the radio, Greff works singlemindedly on the construction of a mechanical contraption resembling a large balance scale. On this he eventually hangs himself by causing exactly his own weight in potatoes to roll down into baskets suspended from the opposite end. When he sees Greff dangling, Oskar senses he is in the presence of the most primal evil, and he imitates the sound of potatoes dropping into baskets when he drums "Ist die schwarze Köchin da? Jajaja!"

Greff has a long history of using dishonest scales—hence the macabre manner of his death. Trouble with the bureau of weights and measures always ensues. This, together with a summons by the morals squad on charges of pederasty, compounded by the grief he feels at the news of the death on the Eastern Front of his favorite former boy scout, drive him to suicide. In the microcosm of Oskar's street in a suburb of Danzig, then, a tangle of dishonest and perverse behavior leading to catastrophe is linked to the larger question of the fortunes of Germany on the Eastern Front. Weighed in a macabre balance, entangled in a web of dishonest and perverted behavior, Germany is hoist by its own petard, committing suicide amid the complexities of the bizarre war machine it has created. Like Herbert Truczinski, Germany perishes when it attempts a full frontal attack with its phallic weapons on Niobe, the very incarnation of war, that man-and boy-killing evil par excellence.

The demise of the German Afrikakorps coincides with two major illnesses in Oskar's circle—Maria's influenza and Kurt's whooping cough—but the next major development in the war and in Oskar's tale occurs with the Allied landing in Normandy. Oskar arrives there, he claims, on the eve of the invasion, in the company of Master Bebra, a gnome whom Oskar had met for the first time in 1934 behind a circus tent. Bebra's mythical pedigree is perhaps even more unbelievable than Oskar's: he claims the hunchbacked Prince Eugene of Savoy and Louis XIV as his ancestors. He had warned his young friend that "they," the Nazis, were coming and that the only way dwarves can survive under "them" is by being on the rostrum, helping to steer the course of events.

Oskar meets Bebra a second time shortly after the death of his mother and learns that Bebra is working for—and is certainly symbolically linked to—that club-footed moral midget Josef Goebbels, the Nazi minister of propaganda. Bebra and his troupe of dwarves, including the charming Roswitha Raguna, the great Mediterranean somnambulist and for-tuneteller with whom Oskar falls in love—she might be considered a personification of Italy in the Axis alliance—entertain the soldiers at the front. When Oskar meets Bebra for the third time, in the spring of 1943, he joins the company, which is on its way to France.

Oskar gives his first performance in an air-raid shelter in Berlin. As he breaks beer bottles for the enjoyment of the troops, the sounds of the air raid above ground are heard. Soon his glass-shattering voice is replaced by bombs which shatter the lights, providing Oskar the opportunity to comfort the frightened Roswitha, as he claims, by making love to her.

Eventually the gnomes arrive in Paris, where, as Hitler had, they see the sights—standing under the Eiffel Tower reminds a somewhat homesick Oskar of being under his grandmother's skirts—including the tomb of Napoleon, with whom Hitler and these megalomanic midgets all strongly identify.

Oskar refines his program as befitting this city of the arts, turning from ordinary German beer bottles to the destruction of beautiful glass art objects from French châteaus. He organizes his performance from Louis Quatorze to Louis Seize to art nouveau, a sense for the historical lost on most ordinary soldiers, he admits, but appreciated by a few educated officers and Francophile journalists from the Reich—one of whom discretely points out a few small stylistic errors in Oskar's aesthetic arrangements.

This condemnation of German barbarism disguised as erudition continues when the company leaves Paris in the spring of 1944 to tour the Atlantic wall. Their delicatessen picnic against the starkness of the concrete bunker—a kind of theater of the absurd—consists of *fine* food items from all over occupied Europe which could only have been obtained by *gross* violence. As they dine, a party of nuns come along the beach looking for crabs for their nearby kinder-garten. Because one of the officers claims the nuns could be British agents, they are machine-gunned in cold blood as the fraudulent picnic merrily continues and the gramophone intones the strains of "The Great Pretender," Oskar's theme song.

The soldier who is ordered to pull the trigger is Pfc. Lankes, an artist who has decorated the bunkers knowing that their concrete will last for thousands of years. The title of his art work, "Mystical, Barbaric, Bored," will serve as the epitaph of our debased culture, he no doubt correctly believes. Oskar apparently concurs with him, for he pens a poem about the nadir of civilization with the refrain "wir nähern uns dem Biedermeier!" (the trend is toward the bourgeois-smug! (Bt 419)).

Oskar's last performances for the troops are certainly the most debased: he breaks a glass chamber pot containing sausages in mustard which Bebra picks out of the glass fragments and eats, much to the delight of the assembled *Übermenschen*. After the last show Oskar goes to bed with Roswitha and is awakened early, as he had been in the Post Office, by the beginning invasion. Roswitha is killed by a shell as she goes for a cup of coffee; Oskar has refused to get it for her, thus once again contributing to the death of a loved one.

Oskar travels with Master Bebra as far as Berlin, where they part for the time being. There is one dark intimation that Bebra might be involved in the July 20, 1944, plot against Hitler (Bt 409). In any case Bebra will appear again in the postwar era of Book 3, and he will perform with his troupe in Berlin under Ballet Master Haseloff in the novel *Dog Years*.

Oskar, a sure precursor of destruction, arrives in Danzig, which is as yet undamaged, on the eve of Kurt's third birthday. Now Oskar's fantasy about founding a dynasty of drummers and his *idée fixe* about returning to the womb assume the most bizarre, gnostic dimensions as he imagines himself taking his son Kurt under his grandmother's skirts and into her womb to a truly communal reunion with all his relatives, living and dead. To this labyrinthine vision are added certain elements of Oskar's *imitatio Christi*, including the Trinity, God the Father, the Only Begotten Son, and the Holy Spirit, paralleled by Jan and his son, presumably Oskar, carried by Oskar's mother and born in his grandmother's womb. This latter element, the *imitatio Christi*, and his identification with the Trinity, will occupy Oskar for the next three chapters.

Kurt, of course, fails to appreciate Oskar's gift of a tin drum or to share in Oskar's visions for his future, though he may, inadvertently, partake of Oskar's destructive nature after all: he brutally destroys his drum and bludgeons Oskar when he tries to intervene. Oskar links this attack with reports of the death in battle of Stephan Bronski and Fritz Truczinski, whose mother has a stroke at the news, all of which causes Maria to seek solace in religion and take Oskar with her to church. When she hesitates at the door, he pulls her inside.

While she waits before the confession booth, Oskar examines his double, the plaster statue of Jesus, and once more places his drum on Jesus' lap. Then, to his great surprise, Jesus begins to play, Oskar claims—others in the church somehow fail to notice it—and, after asking Oskar three times if he loves him, Jesus finally says, "Thou art Oskar, the rock, and upon this rock I will build my church. Follow me!" (Bt 444).

Oskar resists the calling, returning to the church again and again late at night in search of a confirmation of it, apparently concerned that an *imitatio Christi* might take away the glass-shattering power of his voice. After he tests it successfully on some old light bulbs, however, he seems to be satisfied and acquiesces in his new calling, making the Dusters his first disciples.

He meets them late one night when he leaves the church and walks, appropriately enough, along the Adolf-Hitlerstrasse breaking out streetlights and windows. Twenty or so teen-agers follow and eventually corner him on the grounds of a chocolate factory. When they ask him where he comes from, he replies, "From the church." When they ask his name, knowing that the word Oskar will cause them to laugh, he says it is Jesus. Just as they are about to subject Oskar to a painful procedure known as dusting—hence the name of their gang—and just as Oskar repeats his claim to be Jesus, all the air-raid sirens in the city begin to sound, like archangels, Oskar says, taking up and confirming his proclamation of this glass-shattering good news.

Then he gives the Dusters an exhibition of his powers by breaking all the windows in the factory as night fighters and flak shoot down an Allied bomber. His destruction of the windows corresponds with—and is possibly actually attributable to—the air battle. In any case the members of this anarchic gang of delinquents, a *reductio ad absurdum* of wartime society, are impressed, recognizing in Oskar a kindred destructive spirit, the *Wunderwaffe* (miracle weapon) personified, as Oskar calls himself. They invite him to join them as a kind of mascot, or, as Oskar views it, as their Jesus.

When long-range V-1 and V-2 rockets home in on England in the fall of 1944, Oskar sends his long-range voice out from his window to break glass in distant buildings, including the museum where Niobe is housed, so that the Dusters can gain access to steal or take revenge. Oskar denies any responsibility for the murders allegedly committed by the Dusters, including that of over a hundred young recruits horribly burned to death in a docked submarine tender. But he reminds us in this very passage that he, "their spiritual mentor, might have inherited a predisposition to arson from my grandfather Koljaiczek" (Bt 465).

We learn later in *Local Anaesthetic* that his group did commit these murders—possibly without Oskar's knowledge. Oskar says he is certain they were committed by a working-class branch of the Dusters that had Communist leanings and had split off from his group when Oskar influenced them to begin work on his major coup. This project is the creation and furnishing of a church in their hideout in the basement of one of the boy's homes, the von Puttkammer villa (another of several links to the July 20, 1944, plot involving General von Puttkammer, the boy's father). His coup, which also happens to coincide with the Battle of the Bulge, Oskar mentions, involves burglarizing churches and assembling the assorted statuary in the villa.

Soon they are ready for the main pieces: the Madonna and the drumming Christ Child. They manage to saw the Child off the lap of the Virgin.

34

But some of their members have not yet arrived at the church and suspicions arise that Luzie Rennwand, the sister of two of the boys, may have alerted the authorities. To take their minds off their worries, Oskar ascends to the statue and has himself placed in the Virgin's lap. A vandalistic Black Mass ensues with Oskar, the object of worship, accompanying the boys on his drum.

When the police arrive, they find the boys kneeling before Oskar. Luzie Rennwand has indeed, it appears, denounced them. Thus she becomes for Oskar another female incarnation of the Black Cook, the evil principle personified, whose triangular "pubic" face will in the future figure prominently in his paranoia. Störtebeker, the actual leader of the gang and a character in subsequent Grass novels, turns out to be the son of the police chief, Oskar learns to his satisfaction.

Oskar reverts to his old act from the Polish Post Office, pretending to be an innocent kidnapping victim, though Luzie's testimony at the trial—the second trial of Jesus, as Oskar refers to it—threatens to expose him. He manages to survive this trial, however, and we will see him survive yet another trial, the third trial of Jesus, for the murder of a nurse in postwar Düsseldorf, by his same pretence of ignorance and innocence.

On several occasions Matzerath had been urged by Nazi health officials—and by Maria—to have Oskar committed, but he had resisted out of respect for his late wife, Oskar's mother. After the trial, however, an officer apparently connected with the euthanasia program hands him a document and urges him to

35

sign it. The officer's reasoning, with its reference to the Dusters—"You see what kind of elements abuse such a helpless creature"—is itself a ghastly double entendre since the Nazis are the "element" who want to kill Oskar (Bt 478). Matzerath hesitates for ten more days before signing the papers and mailing them to the Ministry of Health.

Oskar's life is spared, ironically, by the fact that Danzig is by this time under Soviet artillery bombardment, and the mail is undeliverable. At first everyone in the house goes to the cellar, including Maria's mother, who is immobilized by her stroke and must be carried downstairs on a chair. Later, however, apparently because it is easier, she is left alone upstairs by her window and is killed by shrapnel.

A crude coffin is made from margarine crates, and she is taken on a handcart to be buried in a park because columns of retreating German tanks have blocked access to the cemetery. Oskar notices that in all the trees lining the streets dangle the hanged corpses of German soldiers, the very young and the very old, who had attempted to desert. Luzie Rennwand's corpse was not among them, he ascertains. Evil is still on the loose.

As the city burns in a great fire storm—an arsonist's dream, Oskar thinks—Matzerath, like a child beginning to doubt the existence of Santa Claus, the Heavenly Gasman, begins to express his doubts about the *Endsieg*, the final German victory. The widow Greff advises him to take off his Party pin, which he does, but he is unable to find a place in the cellar to hide it so he throws it to the floor. Oskar picks it up to prevent Kurt from getting it, he says, but the open pin pricks his hand so he attempts to pin it to the back of Matzerath's jacket. Just at this moment Russian soldiers break into the cellar.

One begins to rape the widow Greff and others play with the children while they wait their turn. Oskar is fascinated by a column of ants on the floor that had found some sugar and by the lice—both entomological microcosms—on the collar of the soldier holding him. He hands the Party pin to Matzerath so that he can have both hands free to catch a louse. Matzerath takes the pin, places it in his mouth, and attempts to swallow it. When it sticks in his throat the Russian soldier empties the magazine of his machine gun into Matzerath. As his presumptive father "swallowed the Party and died" (Bt 489), Oskar crushes a symbolic louse between his fingers. The ants, too, oblivious to the death or to the demise of Nazism simply find a new path around Matzerath's corpse.

A lengthy discourse follows on the history of much-beleaguered Danzig and its destruction over the centuries by many nationalities: historical evidence, to Oskar, that the evil, destructive principle is not a recent phenomenon, nor is it limited to one nation.

This discourse is linked to an account of Herr Fajngold, a Polish Jew who had survived the extermination camp at Treblinka, where his wife and six children had been murdered (along with his sister and brother-in-law and their five children). Fajngold was not killed because he had the job of strewing lime on the corpses and disinfecting the camp.

Fajngold takes over the grocery store, hires Maria

to run it, and helps move Matzerath's corpse out of the cellar where it has lain for three days. Because he speaks Russian and has a pass, he agrees to accompany the party to the cemetery at Saspe, where Matzerath's competitor, Jan Bronski, is also buried. As usual during burials in *The Tin Drum*, airplanes, the angels of death of a technological age, take off and land from nearby airfields.

At the cemetery Oskar tells us he tried to decide whether to begin growing again. He is an orphan now (he believes that Matzerath may have been his father after all, and he confesses he actually opened the Party pin before handing it to him, so the Russians would find it), twenty-one years old, and perhaps ready to lead a more normal life. He throws his drum into the grave and begins to grow, something accompanied by a serious nosebleed.

When the visionary Schugger Leo sees him, he cries, "Behold the Lord, how he grows!" and runs off across the field (Bt 505). This prompts the Russian soldiers nearby to machine-gun him as Oskar, the symbol of helpless, defeated Germany, "in Ohnmacht fiel" (became unconscious, literally: impotent, powerless).

Near the beginning of the next chapter, entitled "Disinfectant," Oskar's pen apparently slips, and he mentions that a stone thrown by Kurt had hit him on the head—just after he had already decided to grow, he still insists—knocking him after his drum into Matzerath's grave. Oskar denies the causal link, citing his previous experience as a three-year-old as evidence that he simply wills his growth to stop or start. But it is clear this is the cause of the nose-

bleed, the *Ohnmacht*, and the subsequent growth,
which leaves Oskar misshapen, a slightly taller
hydrocephalic hunchback, now incapable of doing
any damage to glass with the previous *Wunderwaffe*
of his voice.

Oskar also has a fever, presumably connected with
the lice transmitted to him by the Russian soldiers,
against which Fajngold, the disinfector of Treblinka,
diligently applies Lysol and all manner of other anti-
septics. When an exhausted physician is finally
found, she tells the family about the death she recently witnessed of four thousand refugee children,
and she advises taking Oskar to the West as soon as
he can travel.

In his fever-induced hallucinations Oskar imagines
himself among those children on a great global carrousel with Heavenly Father paying for one ride after another, even though the children are all crying
and frightened and want the carrousel to stop so they
can get off. In this powerful symbolic evocation of
postwar theological nihilism, as Oskar passes him
with each turn of the merry-go-round, Heavenly
Father bears the features now of Rasputin, now of
Goethe, now of a madman surrounded by extremists,
now of a rational moderate surrounded by the forces
of order.

When trains begin running again, when Oskar's
fever abates, after Maria turns down a marriage
proposal from Fajngold, and after Oskar's grandmother comes to see him one more time, Maria,
Oskar, and Kurt finally depart in a freight car for
the West. Oskar is forced to dictate this final chapter
of the war era to his nurse Bruno, since his own fin-

gers swell and his joints ache and grind in sympathy with the growth that occurs during this trip. When Bruno measures him at the conclusion of his three-day confession, Oskar has grown another two centimeters. (Would he and Germany grow to a normal size someday if *all* the truth were told without reservation and hedging?)

The perspective of a third-party eyewitness to Oskar's behavior—there are two such inclusions, that of Bruno here and that of Oskar's friend Vittlar later—provides an interesting test of Oskar's credibility. Also interesting is that Bruno is an artist of sorts who knots ordinary string (in German *ordinär* also means vulgar) into "ghosts, contorted in many layers" (Bt 9). These he immobilizes by dipping them in plaster of Paris and pinning them with knitting needles to small wooden pedestals.

These Giacometti-like sculptural creations depicting various aspects of Oskar's narrative are objective correlatives of that contorted, vulgar, ghostly narrative itself. Their titles are revealing: Bruno calls the landscape in which the figures stand "Europe," for example. He also universalizes by creating groups with titles in the plural—"People on the Rostrum" and "Standing People who Disinfect Reclining People in the Camp at Treblinka" (Bt 522). Hence his reproduction of Oskar's trip to the West begins as a single refugee from the East, but it most likely will become a group of refugees, he says, thus making Oskar a typical representative of all displaced persons.

Bruno points out Oskar's inconsistencies, liberally

sprinkling his account with qualifiers such as the German modals *sollen* and *wollen*, which here mean "is said to" and "claims to." One of Oskar's claims is that among the other people in the car there was a young woman named Luzie Rennwand. After Bruno cross-examines him about it several times, Oskar admits that the young lady's name was actually Regina Raeck, but he continues to refer to her triangular face and call her Luzie.

Her uncle, suffering from stomach cancer, insists he was a Social Democrat before Hitler, and he protests when a Polish officer places two women and six more children in the car. The officer slaps his face, saying he had been forced to live in various places in Germany during the war and had never heard that term. The implication is that many who had supported or tolerated fascism were now overnight self-styled Social Democrats, antifascists, or even resistance fighters.

Gangs of Polish youths frequently stop the train and rob the passengers. Four nuns hold up their crucifixes, which impresses the boys greatly, Oskar recalls: they cross themselves before proceeding to rob the train. When the Social Democrat shows them a document proving he was a paying member of the party from 1931 to 1937, they are equally impressed: they steal his luggage *and* his overcoat. Their leader, who reminds Oskar of Störtebeker, starts to take Maria's knapsack containing the ruby collar—hidden in a packet of Lysol—which Oskar had helped Jan steal for his mother. It also contains his treasured Rasputin/Goethe edition and the photo album. Oskar

41

opens the album and shows the young man a picture of his grandmother. For whatever reason—perhaps he is reminded of his own grandmother—this "Störtebeker" drops the knapsack and takes someone else's luggage instead.

Eventually the Social Democrat dies from a kick in the stomach he receives when he foolishly tries to prevent the theft of his cheap suit. Oskar is also in great pain as he grows, suffering from seizures, a high fever, and from hallucinations about Luzie. When the train arrives in West Germany, he is taken to a hospital in Lüneburg, then to Hannover, and finally to Düsseldorf, where Maria's sister Guste lives. In his fever Oskar apparently ascribes to the nurses and to their white clothing the complementary symbolic meaning of that ascribed to the Black Cook or to the triangular, pubic face of Luzie Rennwand.

The pure, white nurses remind him of his fallen virgin mother, who was a nurse's aide in the hospital when she met Matzerath. The red cross on their white uniforms reminds him of his role as Jesus, of the colors on his drum, of the Polish national colors, and of the color of fire, which so inspired his arsonist grandfather.

Bruno is bored by Oskar's endless stories about nurses, however, and refuses to record what he calls all those banalities. Oskar's fixation on nurses will prove to be an important link between the past and the present; between the death of his mother, for example, and the death of the nurse whom he is accused of murdering.

Book 3: The Postwar Years

In May 1946 Oskar is released from the hospital to begin a new adult life in, and as a symbolic personification of, postwar German society in the era of Konrad Adenauer. Since this Catholic chancellor is kept in power by the Christian Democrats and Bavarian Christian Socialists, popularly referred to as *die Schwarzen* (the Blacks) after the color of clerical vestments, Oskar is still living under the symbolic spell of the Black Cook. She, as we shall see on the last page of the book, casts her black shadow over his entire life.

It is also significant that the first part of his narrative concerns another important symbolic institution of those years before the currency reform, the illegal *black* market. Arriving home from the hospital, Oskar finds Kurt and Maria dealing in cigarette-lighter flints and artificial honey, respectively. Maria rather bluntly urges Oskar to begin on the black market, to help pull his weight in the family.

But Oskar, who at first spends his time discussing collective guilt at the British Center and catching up on his education in evening school and at the theater, is soon drawn back to his preoccupation with death and Jesus. In the course of his long walks he spends time around a cemetery and a nearby monument firm belonging to a certain furuncular Herr Korneff, where a particular statue of Jesus reminds him of the one in the church in Danzig and of Jan Bronski. Oskar expresses his desire to be an apprentice stonecutter there and Korneff, who is apparently desperate for help, agrees to hire him despite his small stature.

To placate Maria, angry because he contributes so little to the family's living expenses, Oskar takes his ruby collar from its Lysol package and exchanges it on the black market for a real leather briefcase and fifteen cartons of American cigarettes—a veritable fortune in postwar Germany—which he gives to Maria in exchange for his room and board. In this way the illegal beginnings of postwar prosperity and the crass materialism that became known as the economic miracle are linked to the evil past of the Crystal Night and to the fall of Germany. Even though the ruby collar has been thoroughly disinfected—that is, denazified by the Lysol, Oskar assures us, this itself further serves as a link to the extermination camp at Treblinka.

In fact, Oskar's narrative goes to some trouble to show that all present phenomena are linked to the past and tainted by it. When Oskar goes with Korneff to deliver a headstone to another cemetery across town, for example, he encounters a postwar reincarnation of the ghoulish psychotic Schugger Leo, this time named Sabber Willem (William Slobber). (Oskar has certainly not lost his sense of the grotesque: he and Korneff leave their dinner pails at the crematorium to be warmed, an act recalling the Germans cooking their meals with gas containing the evil essence of Niobe and supplied by the Heavenly Gasman.) To the accompaniment of the prayers from a neighboring burial, Oskar the Jesus figure resurrects the symbolic contents of two ripe

44

boils on Korneff's neck—the disgusting correlative of Oskar dredging up the buried past—who afterward lies across the tombstone "flat and saved," muttering "Amen" (Bt 555).

During one such trip to deliver a stone to a cemetery on a hill overlooking a large power plant called Fortuna Nord, the local grave diggers, including another Schugger Leo figure, are in the process of exhuming the body of a woman from a neighboring grave. Oskar walks over to inspect the process, a spade still in his hand, which he goes to the trouble of informing us is a former Nazi Labor Corps spade. Onto this former Nazi spade he takes the corpse's middle and ring fingers, which had been cut off by the careless grave diggers. Standing in the cemetery holding the resurrected human fingers on his Nazi spade, Oskar experiences a morbid epiphany. In his ears are the sirens of the plant surging with explosive power, he says, as well as the humming of the high-tension lines overhead, which he describes as the singing of high-tension angels.

Oskar's flashback of death is written in the same panic-stricken style as the chapter on faith, hope, and charity. It combines elements of his wartime Danzig experience—air-raid sirens and explosive angels of death overhead; the death and burial of his presumptive fathers and of his mother; blood-soaked letters in the Polish Post Office; Maria; Luzie; Fajngold; the four thousand dead children—with his more recent experiences in the theater: he sees himself as a resurrected Yorick contemplating Hamlet's corpse.

This morbid resurrection is a metamorphosis of the religious faith in the Hitlerian Heavenly Gasman

45

into a postwar faith in something like an Adenaue-
rian Heavenly Electricityman or Industryman: "Pray
and work—industry and religion hand in hand,"
Oskar intones (Bt 566).

As a result of his epiphany Oskar appears convinced that Germany and he himself, as its proxy,
have returned or are in the process of returning to
their old potency, geopolitical and sexual, respectively. For this reason he apparently decides to propose
marriage to Maria. His previous "love affair" with
her had symbolized the global ambitions and failures
of wartime Germany and its faith in the false god
without whom the people could not cook. Now his
proposal—linked as it is to the economic miracle, to
reindustrialization and to re-militarization—symbol-
izes postwar Germany's equally ambitious and
perhaps equally deadly faith in a new false god without whom they cannot cook: the god of productivity
and of rearmament. Maria politely asks for time to
mull it over, and finally, Oskar says, his question
was answered by the currency reform which takes
Germany further along the road to the *Biedermeier*,
that important symbol of the cultural nadir previously celebrated in Oskar's poem composed at the Atlantic wall.

Before Oskar joins the *Biedermeier* proper by becoming fabulously wealthy as an artist, he must
associate with other artists and become one himself.
This is accomplished after he loses his job with Korneff and becomes a model at the Düsseldorf Art
Academy. The reactions of the visual artists who
variously draw, sculpt, and paint Oskar's dwarfish
person provide for readers of the novel some of the

clearest clues to his role in this literary work of art. Oskar models first for the class of Professor Kuchen, a graphic expressionist whose exclusive medium is black charcoal on white paper. Kuchen, Oskar recounts, "maintained of me that I, Oskar, express the shattered image of man, accusingly, challengingly, timeless, and yet expressing the madness of our century" (Bt 573). Kuchen's students draw Oskar as a personification of his time, as a starved refugee before ruins, as a prisoner before barbed wire and watchtowers.

When he is discovered by the painters and appears in their medium, "Oskar's fresh complexion, his wavy brown hair, his fresh mouth well supplied with blood withered, shimmered in macabre tones of blue, except that here and there, accelerating the putrefaction, a mortally sick green, a nauseous yellow pushed in between chunks of blue flesh" (Bt 580). These artistic efforts tend in the right direction, but it is finally the painter Raskolnikoff—so-called because he constantly mutters "crime and punishment"—who is to capture most successfully the quintessential postwar Oskar. Posing Oskar with a girl named Ulla, known as the muse, Raskolnikoff always senses a vacuum between Oskar's hands. This he variously attempts to fill with a pistol, an hourglass, a convex mirror, scissors, and fish bones. When he finally brings the tin drum, Oskar screams "'Nein!' Raskolnikoff: 'Take the drum Oskar, I have seen through you!' I trembling: 'Never again. That's past.' He, darkly: 'Nothing is past, everything comes again, crime, punishment, more crime!'" (Bt 586).

Ulla the muse, who also incites Oskar to acts of

violence, now kisses him, leaving him no choice but to take up his drum. And so, as a violence-prone, drumming, hunchbacked Christ Child on the left thigh of the nude Ulla, Oskar makes his first public debut in a work of art: "Madonna 49." The painting is widely exhibited before being purchased by an industrialist from the Rhineland. There it now hangs in a board room, influencing the directors and reinforcing the connections made at Fortuna Nord between messianic fixations in the deadly past and those in the industrial postwar present.

Oskar had met the muse Ulla for the first time during a Mardi Gras party at the Art Academy, which he attends dressed as Yorick the fool—albeit lacking a king to be a fool to, Oskar laments. She is in the company of none other than Pfc. Lankes, the decorator of the bunkers in Normandy. Later, as described in the chapter "On the Atlantic Wall, or the Bunkers Cannot Shed Their Concrete," Oskar and Lankes return to the scene of the invasion. There they find the retired officer Herzog, the fanatic who had ordered Lankes to shoot the nuns, now possessed by the idea that the German soldiers could have repelled the invasion if they had been sober at the time. (The idea is reinforced in *Local Anaesthetic* by the unreconstructed character of old General Krings, a manufacturer of cement, that most permanent of materials, who reenacts all the battles of World War II in a mechanized sandbox to discover by what perfidy the predestined victory of the Master Race had been betrayed. Similarly, in *The Flounder*, Grass has a deceased Friedrich II of Prussia reenact his battles in a sandbox in heaven.)

The brutal Lankes does not shoot any nuns this time, but with somewhat the same result he does seduce a young novice who then swims out into the ocean in what Oskar fears may be an attempt to drown herself. Lankes and Oskar fantasize about a new holy war against England with nuns in place of sailing ships, an idea which prompts Lankes to begin painting nuns in this vein and successfully marketing his paintings to West German industrialists, presumably like the one with latent mystical, militaristic tendencies who purchased "Madonna 49."

Since Maria is angry at him for posing in the nude, Oskar decides to find a new place to live. Even though it is only a converted bathroom, he chooses his new dwelling in part because it has a view of the casket storage area belonging to an adjoining mortuary. Zeidler, his landlord, who resembles a hedgehog, Oskar thinks, has an argument with his wife, quite possibly because he has rented the room to Oskar. In his anger he smashes a number of liquor glasses against the stove and immediately thereafter sweeps up the fragments. Oskar admits he sees himself, the destructive spirit, in the hedgehog, but no one ever saw him *sweep up* glass, he boasts! The most important aspect of his new dwelling is that a nurse, Dorothea Köngetter, who works in nearby St. Mary's hospital, as the hedgehog casually mentions, lives down the hall.

From the moment Oskar moves in, he says, "the mystery which is nurses" tempted, possessed, conquered him (Bt 598). He recounts all the nurses he has ever met. He refers to the red cross on the white uniform as the three drops of blood in the snow from the

49

epic poem *Parzival*. He goes out of his way to ride
with nurses in the tram. He sees movies about
nurses, all the while mentally weaving indecencies
into the plot, he admits. He suggests to Raskolnikoff
that he paint him with Ulla as a nurse, the result of
which is the painting "The Fool Heals the Nurse,"
with Oskar representing guilt and the white uniform
of the nurse representing atonement. (Oskar would
have entitled the painting "Temptation," he says, or
"The Door Handle," because he is always tempted to
try Dorothea's door when he is in the house alone.)

His pathological fixation on Sister Dorothea grows:
though he has never seen her, even the silence in her
room is important to Oskar and described in terms of
the silence surrounding the fateful Niobe figure from
Danzig. When she receives mail from a Dr. Werner
at the hospital, Oskar becomes insanely jealous,
eventually steaming open one of the letters and im-
agining in a polite, businesslike communication a
torrid love letter in disguise. One day, then, when
Oskar routinely tries the door handle of her room, it
opens and he goes in.

He opens her closet, looks at her underwear, and
leafs through the books looking for letters from Dr.
Werner. Then he climbs into the closet and closes the
door as he had done as a child in Danzig. When his
hand grips a patent leather belt hanging in the
closet, in the dim light it reminds him of an eel, and
his mind—now *very* deranged—loses itself in free
associations. These involve the phallic black eels
from the black horse's head, which remind him of the
Black Cook as well as the white gulls, like nurses,
covering the black horse's head, which scoop up the

eels and his mother's vomit. All the fantasies are sexually stimulating to Oskar, so with his free hand he opens his trousers and begins to masturbate, an activity—this is not the first time his drumsticks and his penis have been equated—which resembles drumming.

When Oskar has finished, to resolve his stay in the closet playfully, he drums a few loose beats—which he has not done for years, he says—against the inside of the closet. But Oskar would not have begun to drum in earnest again if he had not upon leaving Dorothea's room encountered Klepp, the third boarder in the house of the hedgehog. Klepp is a strange, fat, flute-playing royalist, who stays in his bed for days at a time emitting odors peculiar to a corpse. During their chitchat Klepp asks Oskar if he knows anything about music, whereupon Oskar goes to his room, fetches the drum given to him by Raskolnikoff, and begins to play.

It was the resurrection day of all his previous drums, the Jesus figure Oskar says. Klepp, inspired to play along with Oskar's drummed narration of his life, at the point in the music expressing the hymn-like hope for a miraculous salvation of the lost firebug Koljaiczek, is himself miraculously resurrected from his bed, followed by cadaverous odors. This latter-day Lazarus proceeds to wash: "This transcended a mere washing, this was an ablution," Oskar notes (Bt 630). They go out for an inverted eucharist of blood sausage and beer and agree to start a jazz band.

Klepp's resurrection is accompanied by an immediate conversion from royalism to Communism, faith in which Klepp blends with his other religion, jazz

51

music. Oskar can well imagine that Klepp might also become a convert to Catholicism, for he, Oskar, is prevented only by the bars on his bed from making those three elements, Catholicism, jazz music, and Communism, into his own mystical religion. This will become a reality if Klepp succeeds in having Oskar's trial reopened, thus resurrecting *him* from his bed and from the asylum.

Oskar and Klepp spend their time looking around Düsseldorf's night spots for a suitable guitar player for their band, but Oskar's thoughts are still on Sister Dorothea, whom he has never seen. Finally, in what must be one of the most bizarre and yet most amusing episodes in all literature, he encounters her.

Oskar and Klepp have helped their landlord install a coconut-fiber runner in the corridor. A small remnant of the carpet finds its way into Oskar's room as a throw rug. Late the next evening, full of sausage and beer, he goes to bed nude because his pajamas are in the laundry. After he steps with his bare feet on the coconut-fiber rug before his bed, the prickling, tingling sensation keeps him awake.

Later, when he hears doors opening and closing in the corridor, thinking that Klepp is returning home, Oskar gets out of bed, holds the carpet before him, and goes out into the dark hallway and into the dark toilet. There he encounters the seated Sister Dorothea, who feels only the scratchy carpet, and, if Oskar can be believed, takes Oskar for the devil. He plays along with the masquerade, referring to himself as Satan. When Dorothea faints, he places her on the coconut-fiber runner, lays the mat on her stomach, and attempts to rape her. Oskar claims that the prickly fibers had the same stimulating effect on her as the aphrodisiac fizz powder had on Maria, and soon Dorothea reportedly says, "Come, Satan, come!" (Bt 641).

Oskar, however, finds himself impotent once more (though he still recalls his other sexual encounters as grand exploits). When Dorothea discovers not a virile, hairy Satan but an impotent, naked midget, she rushes to her room and packs. She leaves the house, kicking Oskar out of the way when he tries to cling to her leg. He lies there nude and despondent on the prickly runner waiting for the appearance of his landlord. Only the drunken Klepp's very late arrival with the newfound guitar player Scholle saves Oskar from the full fury of the hedgehog.

The trio leave home at dawn to practice in the meadows along the Rhine. This inspires Oskar to name their band The Rhine River Three. Soon they are engaged by a man named Schmuh, the owner of an establishment called the Onion Cellar, who, when he is upset, comes to the Rhine meadows to shoot a dozen sparrows. The rhythmic report of his rifle blends in with and adds a percussive effect—not dissimilar to that of the tin drum—to their music.

The exclusive Onion Cellar, which with its carbide lamps looks like the potash mine we will encounter in *Dog Years*—the teeth-gnashing actor Matern, one of that book's narrators, is a regular guest—exists to help jaded postwar materialists achieve the emotional release of a good cry. To these denizens of what Oskar calls the tearless century, as he ritualistically hands out kitchen knives and onions, Schmuh is a high priest of weeping, their very savior, Oskar says, for with the liberating tears comes free, open discussion of their problems.

Oskar's drum has always served the same purpose as the onions for him, he says, and one evening he discovers that his drum has a similar but even more powerful cathartic effect on the customers at the Onion Cellar. Like the pied piper he leads them back to their childhood, frightens them with the Black Cook, has them all wet their pants, and then marches them all merrily out the door.

After the death of Schmuh in an automobile accident caused by outraged sparrows, Oskar—whose intuition prompts him not to get in the car with Schmuh—is approached by a certain Dr. Dösch, an impresario who says he had been in the Onion Cellar that night, and who offers Oskar a *Bombenvertrag* (blockbuster contract) for a concert tour (Bt 669). After thinking it over during his trip to Normandy and inspired by Lankes's financial success selling paintings of invading nuns to wealthy industrialists, the hesitant but impecunious Oskar decides to convert his prewar and wartime experiences into the pure gold of the postwar era. He signs the contract, which is with the Concert Agency "West," as it turns out. Before he takes the elevator to their offices in a new high-rise building, Oskar wonders "whether an irritating political matter isn't hidden behind the name of the agency. If there is a Concert Agency 'West' there is certainly also an Agency 'East' in a similar office high-rise" (Bt 687). (Unaccountably, the seven lines containing this quotation are missing from the published English translation.)

That there is something unsavory about this agen-

cy, which as a political symbol smacks of secret
agents representing the capitalistic West, is also reflected three pages later when Oskar compares the
building with a phallus, calling it a box "which
everywhere smelled, looked, and felt to the touch the
same, like something highly obscene which had been
covered by an infinitely stretchable condom, isolating
everything" (Bt 690). (This passage, too, is missing
from the English.)

Arriving on the ninth floor, Oskar almost runs
away from this quintessence of capitalism, of the
military-industrial complex, from the palatial sound-
proof offices with their deep carpets, polished brass,
indirect lighting, cigar smoke, and long-legged secre-
taries. Entering despite his reservations, Oskar is received with open arms by Dr. Dösch and is taken to
see the Big Boss. This turns out to be none other
than Master Bebra, the scion of Dr. Goebbels, now
ancient, ill, and in an electric wheelchair. Bebra reviews the murders of which Oskar is guilty, from
that of Roswitha, through his mother and Jan, to
Matzerath, whose murder Oskar freely admits, not
hiding behind the Russian machine gun as he had
before. Oskar begs Bebra for mercy, but Bebra only
laughs and tells Oskar to sign the contract. As soon
as Oskar does, Bebra rolls away in his chair. Lest
anyone miss the Faustian implications of the pact,
such as selling his soul and incurring the obligation
to do horrible misdeeds, Oskar specifically denies
them.

His disgracefully successful publicity posters,
Oskar says, heralded the advent of a magician, a
faith healer, and a messiah. His entry into the cities

of the Ruhr is described by the verb *heimsuchen* (to afflict, plague, infest, or ravage). He plays before audiences ranging in size from fifteen hundred to two thousand, consisting largely of elderly people in whom he reawakens infantile memories, hopes, and fears.

They cough when Oskar evokes the whooping cough, wet their pants when he imitates a fire storm; and when he evokes the Black Cook for the first time before an audience of hardened miners, they scream so terribly from fright that several hundred windows shatter even behind their thick draperies. Oskar has his glass-shattering voice back (Germany has rearmed?) albeit indirectly through the infantile fears of the (Communist?) bugbear awakened in a democratic majority.

The media make Oskar a cult figure, attribute to him and to his drum *Heilerfolge* (successes at healing, or salvation, also evoking the phrases *Heil Hitler!* and *Sieg Heil!*), and coin the catchword "Oskarism" (Bt 693). On his second concert tour which falls, significantly, during the Advent season, he makes all the people sing a hymn with the portentous text: "Jesus, I live for you, Jesus I die for you." His third tour comes during Mardi Gras, and he changes trembling old grandmas into robbers' molls and shaky old grandpas into robber captains who go "Bang! Bang!" He signs recording contracts. With his wealth and fame, Oskar's reservations about the Agency are gone. Now he and Bebra roll around together in their custom-made electric wheelchairs, though very soon thereafter Bebra dies leaving Oskar as his heir.

With his newfound wealth, Oskar buys Maria a first-class delicatessen grocery in the finest part of town. In return, the materialistic Maria gladly agrees to send away her former employer and suitor in whom Oskar has always resentfully seen his competitor. Klepp moves away and gets married, his Communist sensibilities offended by Oskar's association with the military-industrial complex of Big Capital. Yet Oskar stays in his converted bathroom, and he rents Klepp's and Sister Dorothea's rooms as well, the latter of which he preserves as a shrine.

And now Oskar comes as close as possible to confessing to the murder of Sister Dorothea while at the same time trying not to incriminate himself for it. However, knowing that Oskar is symbolically guilty as the *Zeitgeist*, the quintessence of our murderous epoch, even of murders actually committed by others, and having followed the bent of Oskar's mind for over a half century and half a thousand pages, the reader can, by paying close attention to his narrative, understand how the evil which haunts Oskar all through his life has found a new home in postwar society.

Oskar claims that because he was lonely at home he rented a dog named Lux to accompany him on his walks. In July 1951, he claims, the dog led him to Gerresheim, a suburb of Düsseldorf, and along the grain fields. Unaccountably, Oskar tries to make the dog run out into the fields, but Lux stays close by even after being kicked by Oskar. Finally, Oskar says he was pleased when Lux disappeared into the grain and stayed away for a long time. Oskar sits down on an abandoned cable drum and begins with

two dried sticks to beat out the story of his childhood. Then Lux disturbs him with something in its
mouth which turns out to be a human, female ring
finger complete with a golden ring set with an
aquamarine.

Unnoticed by Oskar, a certain Gottfried von Vittlar has observed the entire episode from his perch in
an apple tree in his mother's nearby garden plot. In
Oskar's mind Vittlar now assumes the role of the
serpent Lucifer—with overtones of St. John the Beloved—for he knows Oskar has found a human finger. Over a year later in a new role as Judas, Vittlar
will notify the police.

Oskar inserts into his narrative at this point a
copy of the deposition filed by Vittlar with the court
in what becomes the most famous case of the postwar
era, the ring finger trial. Vittlar relates at great
length his version of the story, suggesting obliquely
at the outset that Oskar's drumming was motivated
by *das Böse* (Bt 704), the same evil principle that
prompted Oskar to break glass during the era of the
Crystal Night. He and Oskar touch on several political topics, he recounts—a bit later we learn that
they both vote for Adenauer—before Oskar allows
Vittlar to try on the ring. An airplane, that technological angel of death, again flies overhead, reminding
Oskar of Schugger Leo and the other deaths for
which he is responsible.

Together Oskar and Vittlar go to Korneff's work-
shop to have a plaster cast made of the finger—later
Oskar has one made of solid gold. Vittlar suggests
that since the finger was not his property, Oskar
ought to turn it over to the authorities. With impec-

cable logic—for him—Oskar argues that it is his: because of its similarity to a drumstick, to the scars on
his friend Herbert Truczinski's back, to the spent
cartridge casing from Saspe, it was promised him at
his birth.

Three days later Oskar takes Vittlar to his house,
saying he has a surprise for him. In Sister Dorothea's
former room Oskar has enshrined the ring finger in
alcohol in a glass jar, and he reveals to Vittlar that
he occasionally worships or prays to it. Asking Vittlar, as evangelist, to write down the prayer and to
ask questions about it as he speaks it, Oskar kneels,
beats on his drum, and demonstrates his morbid
catechism.

From this cryptic prayer it emerges that the ring
finger belongs to the left hand of Sister Dorothea—
the ring was a gift of Dr. Werner, it appears—whom
Oskar had known very well, much better than their
one nocturnal meeting in the hall would have permitted. She had returned after the experience,
apparently out of some strange masochistic attraction to evil and to the coconut-fiber rug. She had
accompanied a jealous person, obviously Oskar, into
the fields and was picking flowers when she was killed: "Jealousy but unfounded, sickness but not by her
hand, death but not by her hand . . . picked cornflow-
ers, then came, no, accompanied her before, can't say
more . . . Amen?" (Bt 709).

In this incriminating light Oskar's story that he
rented the dog for companionship becomes doubtful.
A more likely possibility is that he took the dog back
to the scene of the crime hoping it would be able to
sniff out the site of the grave and find the finger

which the murderer hacked off out of jealousy over Dr. Werner, whose ring it bore. (A parallel also obtains to the fingers of the corpse at Fortuna Nord.)

In this incriminating light Oskar's previous erotic fantasy in Sister Dorothea's room takes on a quality of morbid premeditation: he imagines meeting Dorothea "under a warm, calm summer sky amid fields of waving grain," (Bt 609) each detail of which is literally echoed in the subsequent account of Oskar's walk with the dog. In addition, a threatening thunderstorm specifically links the event through Oskar's drumming on the cable drum to the gravely portentous thunderstorm at his birth.

As if to underscore the symbolic meaning surrounding the postwar resurrection of Oskar's drumming and his renewed role as a reflection of death personified, one final narrative is included by Vittlar in his meandering deposition. This concerns Viktor Weluhn, who lost his spectacles during the defense of the Polish Post Office but who nevertheless managed to escape. Now, in postwar Düsseldorf, he has finally been captured by two Kafkaesque henchmen—they chase him only in their spare time after work—who intend to carry out the superannuated Nazi death sentence, which, because no peace treaty with Poland had been signed, is still technically in force.

For a lark, Oskar and Vittlar have stolen a streetcar and are driving it late at night. The two henchmen stop them and hoist poor Viktor, still without his glasses, on board. They go to Gerresheim, the same suburb where Dorothea was murdered, and stop at the same spot near Vittlar's mother's garden plot, which is chosen as the site of execution. Viktor is bound to the apple tree; just as the henchmen raise their machine guns, Oskar drums up the ghostly Polish cavalry, which appears as though it consisted of string figures bound by Bruno the male nurse. The cavalry takes away to the East the three specters from out of the past.

When Vittlar congratulates Oskar on his success at conjuring up the cavalry, Oskar, the quintessential reflection of the evil times, implies by his rejoinder that it is the *prevention* of evil which would be worthy of congratulation, but this would require much effort: "I've had much too much success in my life. I'd like one time not to have any success. But that is difficult and requires much work" (Bt 717). Vittlar, missing the deeper symbolic point, insists that he would like to do something like Oskar to get his name in the newspaper, whereupon Oskar invites this Judas to take the ring finger and go to the police with it.

Oskar, then, in order to make the whole affair more valuable to Vittlar, he says, decides to flee. For political reasons he is unable to flee where he would really like to, back to the East, under the skirts of his grandmother, so he heads west in the direction of his grandfather in America. The Agency has provided him with visas for France and for the United States, so he goes via Paris. Because every flight needs to be motivated by fear, a laughing Oskar tries to recall what it is he is most afraid of. The drumming of the train wheels on the rails seems to answer for him: "Ist die schwarze Köchin da? Jajaja!" Before he arrives in Paris he is suffering from mortal terror.

61

In Paris he takes the metro in the direction of the airport but decides to get off at Maison Blanche instead. (Does the name suggest to Oskar "the White House," the very center of the capitalistic world?) The rhythm of the escalator takes over the refrain from that of the subway and of the railroad: "Ist die schwarze Köchin da?" and Oskar answers: "Jajaja!"

Oskar attempts to assign mythical meaning to his ascent on the escalator: he sees himself as Dante returning from Purgatory, as Goethe returning from the mothers. Then, as he slowly ascends, he calls the process ascending to heaven, and Oskar begins to rehearse in a litany the stations of his life, his *imitatio Christi*, ending with "Amen." At the top of the escalator, on the Avenue d'Italie when officers from Interpol arrest him, he says in German, French, and then English: "I am Jesus!"

Two years later, as the novel ends, from his asylum bed Oscar is recounting his flight and his arrest. He is celebrating his thirtieth birthday. Vittlar, the Tempter, has just reminded Oskar that Jesus began gathering disciples at thirty. Oskar's lawyer enters the room and announces that his trial has been reopened. A certain nurse named Beate, who was jealous of Dr. Werner and Dorothea and had been suspected of murdering them both, is now considered to be the real murderer.

Oskar will soon be free, but the fear of the Black Cook from the narrated past grips Oskar anew in the narrative present: he sees himself forced (nailed down) to become a messiah again, to collect disciples and found a sect, a party, or a lodge. What will the future hold for him?

He will, he says, evoke the Black Cook on his drum and query her; for that black evil, that *Kinderschreck* (frightener of children) who cast her shadow at every turn along his path—here Oskar writes a sentence over a page in length summarizing the entire novel—is not behind him in the past anymore but is coming toward him, out of the future, growing blacker and blacker. This prospect is more frightening, he implies, than any he has experienced even in *his* horrifying past: "Ist die schwarze Köchin da? Ja—ja—ja!" (Bt 734).

NOTES

1. See, e.g., Edward Diller, *A Mythic Journey: Günter Grass's "Tin Drum"* (Lexington: The University Press of Kentucky, 1974).

2. See Werner Maser, *Adolf Hitler,* 7th ed. Munich: Herbig, 1978, 35.

CHAPTER TWO

Cat and Mouse
Katz und Maus

LOOKING BACK ON THE CREATION OF *THE TIN DRUM*, Grass admits to having been obsessed. From the moment he wrote its first sentence, he recounts, the characters of the novel, a wildly expanding family, came to life for him and sat around his typewriter (AL 94). For his real family, his wife Anna and their twin sons, Franz and Raoul, born in 1957, he was present during these years less as a husband and a father than as a cloud of tobacco smoke.

Partly for health reasons Grass left Paris for Berlin in 1959 after *The Tin Drum* appeared. A heavy smoker, Grass had written the book in the damp ground floor studio which doubled as the furnace room of his flat on the Avenue d'Italie. Now he discovered he had developed tuberculosis.

Grass was also uncomfortable about the nationalist policies of Charles De Gaulle, who had been elected president of France in December of 1958. He was made even more uncomfortable when for some reason he was detained overnight by the French authorities, an experience, he says, that made him downright homesick for the West German police (AL 97). Though Grass has not been very specific about it, this event may have occurred before the completion of *The Tin Drum* since it corresponds with Oskar's account of his arrest in Paris on the Avenue d'Italie at Maison Blanche, the metro stop closest to Grass's flat at number 111.

Before he left Paris for Berlin, Grass had written a ballet entitled "Five Cooks" produced in Aix-les-Bains and in Bonn, as well as a radio play entitled "Thirty-two Teeth," broadcast by South German Radio. A one-act play "Only Ten Minutes to Buffalo" was produced in Bochum, and a brief curtain-raiser "Beritten hin und zurück" (literally: Mounted There and Back Again, translated "Rocking Back and Forth") premiered in Frankfurt. He had also written more poems, which were to appear in 1960 in a volume entitled *Gleisdreieck* (literally: Three-rail Junction, a railway stop between East and West Berlin).

And he had begun another large novel, a sequel to *The Tin Drum*, under the working title "Kartoffelschalen" (Potato Peelings). In 1963 it was published as *Dog Years*. When one episode from this novel took on its own existence and grew into a separate novella of almost 200 pages, Grass says it helped him solidify his concept and change "Kartoffelschalen" to *Dog Years*. In the meantime, in 1961, he published the novella as *Cat and Mouse*.

Like *The Tin Drum* and *Dog Years*, *Cat and Mouse* is set during the war, in the same microcosm of Danzig, among young people, not a few of whom appear in *The Tin Drum* and again in *Dog Years*. (Störtebeker, the leader of the Duster Gang, returns in

Local Anaesthetic as well.) Oskar is alluded to on one occasion in connection with the arrest of the Duster Gang and on two other occasions puts in brief appearances.

The main character of the novella appears to be Joachim Mahlke, a gangling boy, a devout Catholic, who becomes a tank gunner—like Grass—wins the Knight's Cross, suffers anxiety, probably as a result of battle fatigue, and goes AWOL.

And yet, interesting as he is, Mahlke is only the foil to the real subject of the book: the narrator Pilenz. *He* is the character whose mind Grass seems to wish to explore, a person who sees in Mahlke's life a whole succession of religious symbols. And, like Oskar, it is also the unreliable narrator Pilenz who draws our attention, sometimes apparently inadvertently, to connections between Mahlke's life, these religious symbols, and political, historical events.

Pilenz is the archetypal true believer, a disciple in search of his Jesus, whom he finds or, more correctly, creates in Mahlke. That Mahlke's father is dead, for example, becomes for Pilenz something akin to an immaculate conception. He tells us Mahlke lived in a street called *Westerzeile* (Western Row) and then changes his mind, saying it must have been *Oster-zeile* (Eastern Row, literally: Easter Row [KM 23]). Mahlke's gaunt face and his long hair parted in the middle give him, for Pilenz, a "savior countenance" (KM 147). And when Mahlke plays "Ave Maria" on a gramophone aboard the sunken minesweeper where the boys spend their summers, Pilenz claims it stilled the sea.

When Mahlke becomes a soldier, Pilenz says the

eagle on his army cap "spread itself over your fore-
head as the dove of the Holy Ghost" (KM 147). Pilenz
meets him under a crowning bower, possibly containing thorns, Pilenz recalls, in a castle park. When
Mahlke returns home with the Knight's Cross, Pilenz
sees in it a symbol of the—for him—ineffable cross
and claims that the Virgin had made Mahlke bullet-
proof.

It is a Friday when Mahlke goes AWOL, Pilenz
goes to some trouble to tell us. Then Pilenz describes
a crucifixion, complete with thorns or goads in the
form of unripe *Stachelbeeren* (gooseberries; literally:
thornberries or goadberries), which cause Mahlke in-
tense stomach pains (KM 165). Pilenz himself "nagelte
ihn fest" (pinned him down; literally: nailed him
down [KM 161]). Mahlke goes down to his watery
grave in the old sunken minesweeper in the harbor,
but he does not come up again.

That Mahlke has not come up, has not been resurrected, has been Pilenz's obsession since that significant day in June 1944, corresponding (as we have
seen in *The Tin Drum*) to the Allied invasion. Because Mahlke was a good diver, Pilenz looks for him
in newsreel films about divers. Because Mahlke had
wanted to be a clown, Pilenz visits every circus hoping to see him. And in October of 1959 he travels to
Regensburg to the reunion of the order of the
Knight's Cross. A military band of the *Bundeswehr*
(West German Armed Forces) was playing, he recounts, and during a break Pilenz asks a lieutenant
guarding the door to have Mahlke paged, "but you
didn't seem to want to show up," (literally: to surface
[KM 178]).

Pilenz is ridden with guilt about the demise of his friend, and with good reason: to ensure that Mahlke goes down into the minesweeper, Pilenz cuts off all his escape routes by lying to him. He tells him, for example, that agents in civilian clothes had been at Mahlke's house on two occasions looking for him. When Mahlke asks if his mother was home when this happened, Pilenz extends the lie and feigns sorrow at having to tell Mahlke she had been arrested.

Though it is clear that Mahlke intends to hide in the minesweeper only until dark and then have Pilenz row him across the harbor to what he thinks must be a neutral Swedish vessel and escape from Germany, Pilenz has a more mythical ending in mind. Mahlke dives with his cans of food into the wreck to swim to his old boyhood hideout in the radio shack in a part of the ship's superstructure that is still above water. But Pilenz, the Judas figure, removes his foot from the crucial can opener, a symbol for Mahlke's ability to sustain himself and to free himself from his militaristic metal tomb. And after pounding on the deck and yelling "can-open-er!" for a time, he throws the can opener overboard and rows away. He does not return that evening as arranged, even though he tells the man who rented him the boat that he might, but he looks out the next morning with binoculars at the wreck, where he sees only Mahlke's boots lying abandoned on the deck.

Though it is possible that Mahlke has swum away sometime during the night, it is more likely that Mahlke, ill as he was and weighted down with useless cans of food, drowned before reaching the safety of the radio shack. His plan to escape from Germany may have succeeded, but more likely it was futile, since Pilenz sees no neutral ships in the harbor the next morning. In any case, in his own mind Pilenz has contributed to Mahlke's death, at least mythologically. He is now seeking for a way to atone, seeking a resurrected Mahlke whom he can repay for his perfidy and venerate anew.

An important clue to the meaning of this strange discipleship lies in Mahlke's large Adam's apple, the "mouse" of the book's title. It fascinates the "cat," Pilenz, who says he is forced by him "who invented us for professional reasons," (KM 6) that is, by Grass—to toy with this mouse, take it in hand again and again, and lead it to each locality "which witnessed its victories and defeats." In addition to his odd use of military vocabulary in connection with the Adam's apple, Pilenz, the religious mystic, also relates the growth of this visible symbol of human guilt and of the fall to the beginning of the war in 1939: "Great events were shaking the world at that time, but Mahlke's reckoning of time was: Before he could swim, and: After he could swim" (KM 33).   Before the beginning of the war, Pilenz says, Mahlke had been a sickly child, who could neither swim nor ride a bicycle and was excused from physical education at school. (One is reminded of the fact that the Treaty of Versailles intended to keep Germany weak.) Nor does he show any signs of an Adam's apple. But when Mahlke turns fourteen shortly after the beginning of the war, he begins to be interested in physical prowess and he takes swimming lessons during the winter.

When he swims out to the wreck for the first time the next summer, his Adam's apple is already enormous, at least as described by Pilenz. He calls it "that horrible [fateful, fatal] cartilage . . . which remained extended in the form of a dorsal fin and left a wake" (KM 9). (Oskar had been equally fascinated by Herbert Truczinski's equally portentous Adam's apple a few moments before Herbert attacked Niobe.)

The rest of the book is a record of Mahlke's search for something that will conceal this symbol of guilt. His search finally leads this Jesus figure to his cross, in this case the Knight's Cross. Normally a symbol of military success, here it is a symbol for Mahlke's private and Germany's public military demise. There are two earlier Knight's Crosses in *Cat and Mouse* that lead Mahlke toward his own. The first belongs to an air force pilot who had shot down forty-four Spitfires during the Battle of Britain but who is later shot down himself over the Ruhr. He returns to his old school to deliver a speech in which he romanticizes and glorifies war. After this speech Mahlke begins to desire his own cross. When the next Knight's Cross bearer comes to the school, a submariner whose speech is even more florid and bombastic than the pilot's, Mahlke steals his medal.

For his theft Mahlke is dismissed from his school. He transfers briefly to the Horst Wessel school (named after a Nazi martyr), then he volunteers for premilitary training. Finally, in 1944, he becomes a tank gunner—the air and sea armed forces now offer him less of an opportunity to earn his own cross, he implies. With this succession of Knight's Crosses, the stages of Germany's defeat are described. Initial superiority in the air and under the sea for which the crosses are awarded, changes to inferiority. Germany's land arm, its armor, will be the next, and the last, to crumble.

The tanks point to another important element in Pilenz's fixation: the phallic. On several occasions Pilenz allows a glimpse of the fact that whereas he himself is impotent—a condition connected to his having been the sexual object of the priest Gusewski—he engages in phallicism of "the Great Mahlke," as Pilenz calls him (KM 97) . During an adolescent masturbation contest on the old minesweeper Pilenz describes Mahlke's penis as "much more grown up dangerous worthy of worship" (KM 40). He says it "permitted an albeit bizarre, nonetheless balanced harmony" with Mahlke's Adam's apple (KM 41).

When Mahlke becomes a tank gunner, the connection between his "dangerous" penis and the phallic tank gun becomes more obvious. While Pilenz rows them out to the minesweeper, Mahlke utters bits and pieces of the speech he had planned to give at his old school. Perhaps because Mahlke is ill and suffering from battle fatigue, he blends into the almost incoherent account of his tank battles his prayers to the Virgin. This suggests to Pilenz, who spends his time reading the gnostics and Christian mystics, that Mahlke was able to destroy so many Soviet tanks because an image of the Virgin hovered in front of them. He simply aimed his phallic gun at her belly, in front of which she held a picture of his dead engineer-father standing next to his locomotive.

What might be viewed simply as stress-induced hallucinations in a Catholic boy—whose father had died a violent death in a railroad accident—becomes in Pilenz's reportage evidence that Mahlke is directed by the Queen of Heaven. Even their approach to the minesweeper, Pilenz says, might have been guided by an apparition of the Virgin: "not for the length of a single oar stroke was I sure whether he saw more than the usual gulls above the looming superstructure of the bridge" (KM 170).

This linking of the Virgin with the war, the linking of true belief in heavenly apparitions with true belief in the manifest, divine destiny of a political system, reminds us of Oskar's incendiary grandfather, inspired by the Virgin to start fires against his political enemies. It also reminds us of the final long sentence of *The Tin Drum*, where Oskar spies the Black Cook "also behind the high altar—what would Catholicism be without the Cook, who blackens all confession booths?" (Bt 733). Oskar then proceeds to apply to the Black Cook all the words traditionally connected to the worship of the Virgin: "Blessed Virgin, Mother of Sorrows, Sanctified Virgin, Holy Virgin of Virgins." Pilenz's and Mahlke's fixations correspond to those of the impotent Oskar's fixation on himself as a messiah—and on the messianic greatness of his penis—as well as on all the "virgins" in his life: his mother, Maria, and all the black nuns and white nurses, right down to the Black Cook.

In the final analysis, then, *Cat and Mouse* appears to be a psychological study in impotence and in discipleship, a study of a true believer who sees in the person of a boyhood friend a higher, mythical personification, perhaps of Germany, certainly of Germany's guilt and demise toward which he feels he contributed. In his restless seeking to understand this guilt and demise, he resembles no one so much as the author Günter Grass himself, with whom Pilenz, not just Mahlke, shares some common traits: Pilenz is a volunteer at an antiaircraft battery, for example, and is later involved in a battle near Cottbus. But, like the other narrators of Grass's works, such as Oskar, Pilenz is also a pathological case, or the *Zeitgeist* of a pathological time, a reflection and at the same time a personification of its flaws.

Thus when Pilenz goes to Regensburg in October 1959 to the reunion of Knight's Cross recipients, seeking Mahlke, he must stand for all those who go there, true believers seeking a remnant of their Nazi past, seeking a celebration of a supposed glory which was in reality a calamity. That the event is now supported by the *Bundeswehr* is a bitter indictment by Grass of postwar militarism, a powerful statement that there are those in the *Bundeswehr* seeking a resurrection of the old, messianic glory of the Nazi era. These sexual duds, Grass implies, seek in the mysticism of phallic gun barrels the fulfillment they cannot attain in normal life.

CHAPTER THREE

Dog Years
(Hundejahre)

IN 1961, THE YEAR HIS DAUGHTER LAURA WAS BORN,
another of Grass's plays, "The Wicked Cooks," was
produced in Berlin. But Grass continued to concen-
trate most of his literary efforts during this period on
his new novel, *Dog Years*. It would eventually grow
to nearly 700 pages, almost exactly the same length
as *The Tin Drum*. In this massive collage of fantasy
and historical reality Grass continues to develop the
themes, the localities, the characters, and the narrative techniques of *The Tin Drum* and of *Cat and
Mouse*. (These three books were later published
together as the Danzig trilogy.)

Dog Years is structured—even more than the previous works—around Grass's two major personal concerns: art and politics. Specifically, *Dog Years* is
about the role of the artist in understanding how the
politics of the past inform the present and thereby
determine the future.

Dog Years is a complex work. In some ways it may
demand more of the reader than *The Tin Drum*,
which, for all its complexity, is unified by the mes-
merizing mono- and megalomania of Oskar Matzerath. (This may be one reason why critical reaction to
Dog Years seemed relatively restrained: fewer people

seemed outraged by it, and even many of those who had been enthusiastic about *The Tin Drum* seemed rather more baffled by *Dog Years*. With the passage of time, however, it would appear *Dog Years* is actually one of Grass's greatest novels, perhaps even—*de gustibus non disputandum*—his greatest to date. He himself has stated that it is his favorite and his most misunderstood.)

Here there are *three* narrators, the attentive reader eventually discovers. The first is Herr Brauxel, the owner of a former potash mine—in place of potash he now dredges up the past—who also spells his name Brauksel and Brauchsel. He is the third-person narrator of the first of the three books of *Dog Years*. As befitting his occupation, his thirty-two chapters are entitled "Morning Shifts." Book 2 is a first-person narrative written to his female cousin Tulla Prokriefke by one Harry Liebenau, a poet of sorts who once aspired to be a historian, and is subtitled "Love Letters." Book 3 is subtitled "Materniads," after its third-person narrator the actor Walter Matern.

Brauxel is the leader of this collective of authors—all of whom have learned their craft from someone who was diligent on lacquered tin, that is, from Oskar—and it is Brauxel who solicits from and pays Liebenau and Matern for their contributions. Brauxel is also, we discover, the *subject* of their writings. He is in reality Eduard (Eddi) Amsel—alias Brauxel, alias Mister Brooks, alias Hermann Haseloff, alias Goldmäulchen (Lil' Goldmouth)—the erstwhile childhood friend of Matern and childhood acquaintance of Liebenau.

Brauxel now induces his two coauthors to write about his—and their—past much as Grass "induced" Pilenz to write about his past in *Cat and Mouse*. From multiple narrative points of view, then, a unified story emerges: the story of two blood brothers growing up in and around Danzig, experiencing the rise of National Socialism, the war, and its aftermath.

And though they are blood brothers—even the pocketknife they use to draw the blood is an important symbol in the novel—Amsel and Matern are also polar opposites. Amsel is sensitive and artistic, a fine singer, portly but skilled at games like *Faustball* (a kind of volleyball) requiring intelligence and finesse. Matern is compulsive, more emotional than rational, physically powerful, and prone to brutality.

Amsel is a half Jew whose wealthy, very assimilated, patriotic father dies at Verdun, having tried to shed his Jewishness with the help of a book written by an anti-Semitic Jewish crackpot named Otto Weininger. Eddi inherits this book, which becomes his handbook of cultural aberrancy, something like Oskar's Rasputin. His mother's later death leaves Amsel a rich inheritance, most of which he places in Swiss banks.

Matern, whose father owns a historic windmill, is Catholic, the descendant of feared robbers and arsonists named Materna. Matern's miller father has the remarkable ability to hear with one otherwise deaf but magically clairaudient ear the whisperings of the mealworms in a sack of flour held on his shoulder. These worms themselves have the uncanny ability to predict the future, a trait that enables the local farmers, through the medium of the miller Matern, to plant and harvest at the right times and to avoid crop failures and falling prices. The worms also accurately foresee, to the day, the beginning of World War II.

At first Matern joins the other children in persecuting Eddi Amsel, and as often as not he is the one who calls Eddi *Itzig!* (Sheeny). Later, however, recognizing Eddi's talent, Matern—called the gnasher because of his habit of grinding his teeth in anger—uses his fists to protect his weaker friend, whose artistic creations and whose Jewishness continue to evoke persecution.

From time to time, however, Matern turns on Amsel again, especially after Matern becomes a Nazi storm trooper. With eight other brown-shirted members of the SA, he beats up Amsel, knocking out all thirty-two of his friend's teeth. Amsel disappears, has his teeth replaced with gold ones—hence the alias Goldmäulchen and the ubiquitous symbol thirty-two—and remains elusive for Matern during the war and thereafter. Then, under the alias Brauxel, he engages Matern and Liebenau to help write his story.

It is the story of a gifted mimetic artist. Like Oskar, Eddi is precocious, and like Grass, he begins as a sculptor. Eddi's unique gift lies in his vision, his ability to see the essence of phenomena and to recreate that essence in sculptures made of castoff junk, the flotsam of prior floods and other calamities which he fishes out of the river Vistula, itself a symbol of the flow of time. His peculiar optical gifts are

77

only intensified by his persecution: even as he is beaten, his tears lend him "blurred and yet overly precise optical powers" (Hj 42).

Two or three days after each such beating, somewhere in the landscape one of Eddi's sculptural creations appears, depicting the very essence of the brutality of his tormentors. Because Matern sees himself depicted as such a statue one day, sees himself ninefold—a premonition of his attack with the other SA men—striking out in blind rage, he turns his fists away from beating Eddi to protecting Eddi. Such is the power of Eddi's vision and of the mimetic expression of his vision in his art.

For practical local farmers in his village, who know little and care even less about art, Eddi Amsel is a manufacturer of scarecrows. His creations are so startling that they have the power to frighten horses, cows, and even people, not to mention the poor birds who fly up in a great cloud at Amsel's christening, covering the sun and casting a foreboding shadow upon him. One old crow is so scared it falls to the ground quite dead. And yet Eddi has nothing against birds. He sculpts what he sees. It is the frightening essence of the things he sees which strikes terror into the hearts of birds, natural creatures highly sensitive—hence their use in mines like Brauxel's— to potential dangers in the atmosphere.

"The scarecrow is created in the image of man," Brauxel's motto runs (Hj 41). Hence it comes as no surprise that Amsel's *Diarium* or sketchbook—later kept in Brauxel's safe and referred to as the *Pandämonium,* the dwelling place of all the demons—is crawling with uniformed scarecrows from every historical period. Around 1933, Amsel becomes obsessed with making brown-shirted replicas of SA men complete with pig-bladder heads, pasted-on faces of celebrities cut from magazines, and a built-in clockwork mechanism that enables them to march and salute.

But Eddi makes models of all the legendary and historical figures of the region: He sculpts the headless nuns and Teutonic knights who first conquered the area and now still haunt old mills, inns, and chapels where they hold Christian-pagan Black Masses. He sculpts the legendary milk-drinking eels which crawl ashore in thick fog to drain the cows. He sculpts characters from the wars of religion and religious arsonists, whose present counterparts still fight and set fires for religious reasons. He sculpts the murdered Christian missionary Adalbert of Prague and Napoleon's governor Rapp, both of whom are encountered again in *The Flounder* along with the lethal cooking spoon with which Matern's brutal, teeth-gnashing grandmother is armed. He sculpts the Materna brothers, those medieval incendiaries from whom Walter, doubly descends: his grandmother and his grandfather were cousins, both named Matern.

Eddi gives himself over to mythology and sculpts gods, especially the local Old Prussian deities about whom he learns in school and whom he blends into the Germanic and Christian pantheons: Perkunos, the red god of fire; Pikollos, the white god of the dead; and Potrimpos, the god of fertility. Later, as Brauxel, in his mimetic underground studio/ scarecrow factory, he captures in dynamic, fiery sculptures of these syncretic gods the apocalyptic quintessence of the *Dies Irae*.

Though he concentrates on humans and gods, literally everything in his environment becomes a model for young Eddi. (Dogs are a notable exception, apparently because these animals are ready-made artistic symbols requiring no further sculptural abstraction.) Eddi even creates a giant bird which has the effect of scaring birds. Made with tar and feathers, it is so terrifying that even the farmers are not interested in purchasing it. Hardened fishwives avoid it like the plague, and men allow their pipes to go out as they stare at it. Every misfortune in the village, including the death of Matern's grandmother, is blamed on this Baal, this *Kinderschreck* (frightener of children, like the Black Cook in *The Tin Drum*), this "Great Cuckoo Bird" as one of the superstitious villagers calls it (Hj 102).

Eventually Amsel is told he must destroy the bird and all of his collected raw materials. A great mound is heaped up by eager volunteers, the bird is placed on top, and the whole ignited. As Amsel watches this ritualistic burning—taunted by cries of "Itzig!"—his eyes narrow into "seeing slits," and he has an apocalyptic vision of ritualistic tarrings and featherings (Hj 103). He sees state supported pogroms, autos-da-fé, and holocausts; the ceremonial burning of the bird is called a *Staatsaktion* (act of state). And he sees that when he is older he will be forced to make an artistic copy of this in the form of a giant bird that will burn eternally, "simultaneously apocalyptically and decoratively."

In the meantime, Amsel and Matern have begun to commute to school in Danzig, and soon they move into a boarding school there. Beneath the school

Amsel perceives, with his sense for the hidden and for the subterranean, a network of medieval tunnels where he and Walter find the skeleton of one of Napoleon's dragoons.

At the seashore the boys also encounter Alfred Matzerath singing patriotic Nazi songs. Oskar, of course, is on hand, as is Postal Secretary Jan Bronski. Pilenz and his crowd, who attend the same school, are there, as is Störtebeker. They encounter the trumpet player Meyn and Harry Liebenau. Harry's cousin Tulla is a female member of the Duster Gang and a Black-Cook embodiment with the same triangular face as Luzie Rennwand from *The Tin Drum*. (Additional light is shed on the possible symbolism of the triangular face when Tulla's hate-filled visage is described as triangular in the immediate context of a black, triangular Nazi flag bearing a swastika [Hj 153f].)

Tulla is an important character in *Cat and Mouse* as well, where she functions as a reptilian female temptress for Mahlke. In fact, Tulla is more often described as an animal than a human being. After the drowning death of her brother Konrad, for example, she moves into the doghouse, eats the dog's food, and crawls on all fours for over a week.

In Danzig the brutal and the gentle blood brothers meet their teachers, also mentioned in *Cat and Mouse*. Mallenbrand is a brutal physical education instructor who favors the nationalistic game of *Schlagball* (hitball) over the less violent international sport of soccer. For him *Schlagball* was a *Weltanschauung*, a method of inflicting ritualistic pain on Jews like Amsel. The gentle Brunies is a humanist addicted to Eichendorff and to sweets. He collects special stones containing *Glimmerspiegelchen* (flakes of mica, literally: gleaming mirrorlets). His empty flagpole, during the euphoria surrounding the beginning of the war, calls all the swastika-bearing flagpoles into question.

One summer while the boys and their teachers are on a trip to the school's retreat in the forest, Brunies meets with a band of Gypsies. He regularly does this to trade for wild honey and for his micaceous rocks. This time the Gypsies give him a silver ring named Angustri and a baby girl whom he names Jenny. The foundling becomes the target of Tulla's persecutions. These include locking Jenny in an icehouse overnight, covering her with leeches from a pond, and then cooking the engorged leeches into a soup which (shades of Oskar) Jenny is forced to eat.

Three times, with ever more serious results, Tulla sets her dog on Jenny and on Jenny's piano teacher Felsner-Imbs. On the occasion when Tulla's face is compared to a Nazi flag, as Tulla spits into Jenny's baby carriage, we are reminded of the symbolic nature of Tulla's torments by an approaching thunderstorm and by the presence of Oskar, who has observed the entire matter.

Now the dramatis personae of *Dog Years* has been almost fully described but it could hardly be complete without the dogs. In the dark beginnings there was a Lithuanian she-wolf, we read, whose grandson, the black dog Perkun, sired the bitch Senta, who belongs to the miller Matern, Walter's father. A dog named Pluto is brought from Stutthof, the site of the future death camp, to service Senta, and Senta whelps six pups, among them the male Harras.

Later Senta shows signs of reverting to the violent behavior of her she-wolf ancestress and must be destroyed. In the meantime, however, Harras is purchased by the father of Harry Liebenau to be a guard dog in his cabinetmaking shop. Then, even though Harras also shows signs of atavism, this black creature (he is called priest black, SS black, Falange black, snow black, and—borrowing an image from Paul Celan's famous "Death Fugue" about the extermination camps—milk black) becomes the sire to Prinz, Adolf Hitler's favorite black German shepherd. Many of the proud people in the house by the cabinetmaking shop become Nazis.

On the last day of World War II, the eighth of May 1945, at 4:45 a.m., the exact time of the beginning of the war in 1939, this symbolic dog, having deserted the doomed Hitler, swam across the river Elbe near Magdeburg "and sought on the west side of the river a new master" (Hj 427). The visionary Amsel, sensing early on a historical, mythological symbol (Harras bears the dog license number 517, the sum of whose digits is the unlucky 13), a tie to Herr Hitler, asks permission of Liebenau to sketch Harras. He calls him Herr Pluto, the hound of hell, and uses—unheard of for dogs—the polite form of German address. But Tulla and young Harry Liebenau, Matern later maintains, chase Amsel away by calling him "Itzig!"

Thereafter Amsel begins to make his brown-shirted sculptures, the soiled uniforms for which are obtained by Matern, a former Red Guard thug who, along with many of his old Communist friends, now joins the SA. The stains—blood, beer, sweat, grease, tar—make the clothes valuable to Amsel in whose visionary imagination the stained clothes represent the entire violent Nazi movement. But Matern is unhappy about Eddi's SA men robot/sculptures, especially because of their pig-bladder heads, and, a more subtle matter, their association with the dogs. He accuses Eddi of representing his comrades as *Schweinehunde* (swinish sons of bitches). Amsel replies that he merely reproduces with artistic means what life shows him, and he begins to build a replica of the SA man Matern which mechanically grinds its teeth.

Eddi's artistic view is the correct one, of course, something subtly underscored at this very point in the novel. Harry Liebenau and his cousin Tulla observe Eddi and Oskar Matzerath together in a snowstorm. Their ears are pressed to Oskar's tin drum as they listen in the sound of December snow falling on the drum to what is "in the wind." The beating Eddi accurately predicted when he made the original scarecrow of Walter Matern striking out ninefold in blind anger is now approaching at the hands of Walter and eight of his SA *Schweinehunde* friends.

They beat up Eddi Amsel in his garden, knocking out all his teeth, and roll him into a snowman with a red mouth which grows larger and larger. Not far away, near the black Gutenberg temple on the hill, the sinister specter Tulla, who leaves no tracks in the snow and who also has a windup mechanism in her belly, is making, along with eight of her followers, an exactly parallel attack on Jenny Brunies. The same black crows fly back and forth in the white snow to observe how both of these sensitive artists, the sculptor Eddi and the ballerina Jenny, are beaten, rolled into snowmen—reminiscent of the icehouse assault where Tulla also has eight followers—and left alone by their attackers. And both emerge later from their snowmen when a thaw sets in.

Although they were both fat before, the eyewitness Harry Liebenau swears they were resurrected thin. The visionary Amsel had already depicted Jenny as a thin ballerina in his drawings. He had apparently also anticipated the attack on himself since he has a forged passport ready weeks in advance with the picture of a thin man wearing a pained expression around his mouth. With this in hand he leaves for Berlin under the name Hermann Haseloff. There he gets gold teeth and becomes an important *maître de ballet*, the chief of a propaganda company under Josef Goebbels, entertaining the troops and making strange, hominoid machines in his basement studio. (Later, as Brauxel, because he is understandably pained by the sight of crows in the snow, he considers test-firing the apocalyptic Perkunos, Pikollos, and Potrimpos to burn away the snow and the crows.)

The gentle teacher Oswald Brunies is denounced for eating the sugary vitamin tablets intended for his students. Then, in front of school and police officials at the hearing, Tulla tempts him into grabbing a handful of tablets out of a jar. Harry further incriminates him by mentioning he does not fly the swastika, and Brunies disappears into the death camp at

Stutthof. Thereafter Haseloff comes to Danzig in his black Mercedes and takes Jenny back to Berlin, where she assumes the stage name Jenny Angustri.

Haseloff returns with a truck for Brunies's furniture and collection of micaceous rocks, which he deposits at the site of his future potash mine in Lower Saxony. He also arranges for Felsner-Imbs to become his rehearsal pianist. Around the time of the invasion of June 1944, Haseloff begins to produce a ballet he had been preparing since his childhood entitled "The Scarecrows."

Haseloff's ballet (a version of which would be produced under the same title at the German Opera in Berlin in 1970) employs what remains of the troupe of midgets under Master Bebra with whom Oskar Matzerath had entertained the troops in occupied France, as reported in *The Tin Drum*. Described by Jenny in her letters to Harry Liebenau, the ballet is a fantastic allegory of Germany and of the world. It is a microcosmic artistic reproduction of Amsel's apocalyptic visions, complete with robot scarecrows, a sinister Hitlerian gardener, and a twelve-legged black dog, the hound of hell, all of which ends with the total destruction of the garden. Dressed in rags, only the limping figure of the evil old gardener survives, and he is changed into a scarecrow as the curtain falls.

Two gentlemen from the Propaganda Ministry who attend the dress rehearsal find the plot too sinister and suggestive for the soldiers on the front. "The life-affirming element is missing," they complain (Hj 404). Strings are pulled at the highest level, and Haseloff is allowed to add a socialist-realist happy ending. In it the scarecrows are bound, taken from their underground setting to the surface, and harnessed into the service of the formerly evil, now wonderfully virtuous gardener. Amsel's art has always truly reflected and predicted the consequences of reality, however, so even as the troupe rehearses the new happy ending, a bomb falls on the rehearsal room. It kills Felsner-Imbs and smashes Jenny's feet, thus confirming with a vengeance the correctness of the original finale.

Meanwhile back in Danzig, Matern is involved in more pogroms and possibly in the murder of a dock worker, but like the trumpet player Meyn he is eventually ejected from the SA for a peccadillo, the theft of a small amount of money. He loses an engagement as an actor at the theater in Schwerin because he drinks heavily and spouts anti-Nazi slogans. In his inebriation the Virgin Mary appears to him and commands him to poison the dog Harras. The drunken Matern calls Harras a black Catholic Nazi swine, but he seems to lack the courage to kill him and instead goes to Düsseldorf for a few months. There the inebriate expression of his Communist views gets him thrown out of his athletic club and into jail, where the police break several of his ribs. To escape prosecution he joins the army in the summer of 1939 and is sent back to Danzig.

In August, two days before the war begins and Matern marches into Poland—the ships of the line that fire the first shots of the war have already taken up their positions, we read—he throws poisoned meat to Harras. Harras has been trained not to take food from strangers, but Tulla, knowing the meat is poisoned, urges him to eat it.

When the Führer comes to Danzig a few days later, he invites Harry and his sorrowing father, as the owner of Prinz's sire, to meet him at the Grand Hotel. Hitler does not appear, but they see Prinz, who is, as they proudly note, the exact black image of the late Harras.

On a school visit to the country, Harry Liebenau visits the miller Matern and asks him about the future: "Will we get as far as Moscow?" "Many of us will even get as far as Siberia," the oracle replies (Hj 326).

As the war drags on, Matern, Liebenau, and Störtebeker are assigned to an antiaircraft battery across the marshes from a large white mound. Although crows and rats thrive in the area and a strange odor permeates the air, no one wants to admit this is a mountain of human bones from the death camp at Stutthof that are being processed into glue and soap. Tulla, who herself always emits the infernal smell of bone glue—her father is in charge of the glue pot in the cabinetmaking shop—finally strikes out across the marshes and returns with a human skull.

For revealing the truth, she is rewarded with a slap in the face by Matern, the archrationalizer, who also introduces the others to a strange jargon, a parody of the language of the philosopher Martin Heidegger. Heidegger comes under attack by Matern—who should not be equated with Grass—because Matern, always looking for a scapegoat, claims the philosopher was born the same year as Hitler in a village near Hitler's birthplace. (The former is true, the latter is false, though both are irrelevant.)

This is a language, says Matern, that obfuscated rather than enlightened, that "was an antidote against thinking" (Hj 474), permitting an abstract discussion of Being in the very shadow of a mountain of human bones, allowing the mountain to be buried in medieval allegories. As Matern kills crows and Störtebeker kills rats, they babble: "True, the rat can exist without the ratty, but rattiness can never be without the rat" (Hj 367).

Eventually Matern makes derogatory remarks about Hitler and is sentenced to clear mine fields. He somehow survives, albeit with a limp, but this allows him to claim the status of anti-fascist at the war's end.

Tulla, originally intended by Grass to be Oskar's little sister (AL 94), has an obsession with becoming pregnant, perhaps in a female inversion of Oskar's symbolic militaristic fixation on his potency. She engages in a veritable marathon of promiscuity (Mahlke also claims to have had sex with her) until finally—the most likely presumptive fathers are Matern and Störtebeker—she succeeds. But as the German war effort fails on all fronts, the finger-long fetus spontaneously aborts.

Her cousin Harry, whose love for Tulla is frustrated by his impotence, is finally inducted and travels to Berlin with the sound of her name, like Oskar with the Black Cook, in the train wheels: "Duller Duller, Tulla. Dul Dul, Tulla. Tulla Tulla, Dul" (Hj 409). Harry, the aspiring poet, seeks in vain a rhyme for her name until the tank he is assigned to backs for cover into a wooden shed filled with products from a local glass factory. Only the sound of a tank crushing glass—one is of course reminded of Oskar's voice—rhymes with Tulla.

The cabinetmaker Liebenau realizes what a calamity Adolf Hitler represents, and on Hitler's birthday, April 20, 1944, he takes an ax to Harras's empty doghouse. The house is a proxy for Hitler, and its destruction, we are given to understand, a parallel symbol for the futile bomb planted at the Führer's headquarters by Klaus von Stauffenberg exactly three months later on July 20, 1944.

The dog symbolism deepens: even as Hitler celebrates his last birthday on April 20, 1945, Prinz, the four-legged symbol of death and the evil principle, deserts Hitler, doubling and redoubling into an eight-, twelve-, and then twenty-four-legged symbol as he flees.

Reports of dog sightings and of the dog's whereabouts conflict. An unofficial Swedish report says he has been taken to Argentina (along with how many other high Nazis?) in a U-boat. But when Hitler's will is opened, it reveals he has bequeathed Prinz to the German people. He is *their* legacy.

As we have seen, like all the other Germans fleeing before the Soviet armies, leaving behind their mountains of bones, their mass graves, their party membership lists, their Nazi flags, and their guilt, Prinz swims across the river to the West, seeking a new master. With the words "let no one who can read believe the dog did not arrive," (Hj 427) Liebenau concludes his book. "The dog stands at the center,"

the postwar third book then begins; that is, the dog
stands at the center of postwar life.

The dog finds Matern, this book's author, after his
interview by a Mister Brooks or Braux, an officer of
the occupation army, as Matern is being released
from a British anti-fascist camp. The dog follows him
everywhere despite Matern's attempts to frighten
him away. The violent, irrational Matern, belligerent
Red Front thug turned belligerent SA thug turned
belligerent antifascist, is the new custodian of Prinz,
whom he calls Pluto, the hound of hell.

Matern now limps around Germany as the reincarnation of past violence and the bizarre personification of the denazification process. He plans terri-
ble revenge but metes out only absurd punishments
to relatively innocent people. He strangles a canary
that had survived the bombing raids. He infects with
gonorrhea and is reinfected by willing daughters and
wives of his old comrades and antagonists. He urinates in Heidegger's mailbox. All the while he covers
up the real guilt in his own soul.

Eddi Amsel, however, will not allow Matern to
forget or cover up. In his guises as Brooks, Brauxel,
and Goldmäulchen, he uses a variety of reminders,
such as hiring Matern to write his history. He opens
a restaurant called the Morgue where teeth pudding
is served to a shocked and nauseated Matern. He enters a float featuring headless nuns and knights in
the Mardi Gras parade in Cologne. In short, he artistically dredges up from the mine of memory, from
the depths of the forgetful Matern's own subcon-
scious—even from the bottom of the Vistula, in the

case of the fateful pocketknife—all his evil deeds.
Like the six electrical shocks that finally cure
Matern of his venereal infections (spouting a litany
of Nazi slogans about attacking the Slavic Eastland,
Matern points his *apparatus belli* to the east wall of
a farmhouse and urinates into an electrical recepta-
cle), Brauxel administers a series of therapeutic mnemonic shocks to Matern's, and to Germany's, soul.

One such shock is that caused by the *Wunderbrille*
(miracle glasses) or *Erkenntnisbrille* (perception glasses) which Brauxel & Co. place on the market in
1955. Within a short time exactly 1,456,312 of these
toys (a figure of the same magnitude, probably intended to symbolize the sales of *The Tin Drum* and
Cat and Mouse) are sold to children all over Germany except in those areas known to be politically
reactionary, such as Schleswig-Holstein. There the
glasses are confiscated (and Grass's works were temporarily banned). But in the cities and in the area
around Itzehoe (the site of Grass's home at Wewelsfleth) some glasses are sold.

Made with cheap plastic frames and simple flat
lenses—to the glass of which is added a small
amount of mica chips from Brunies's Gypsy rocks,
making them miniature crystal balls—these distres-
sing and exceedingly controversial eyeglasses impart
to the wearer something of the optical powers of Eddi
Amsel: when children from seven to twenty-one put
them on, as if by magic they see what their parents
were doing during the war. It is not the erotic secrets
revealed by the miracle glasses—there are surpris-
ingly few of these—but the hidden acts of violence,

the murders, the accessories to murder which cause the children distress.

Unwittingly, Matern buys a pair of these glasses for Walli Sawatzki, the ten-year-old daughter of his SA friend Jochen Sawatzki (or perhaps Matern's own daughter, since he has often joined the Sawatzkis in bed). In any case, when Walli puts them on, she goes into shock and must be hospitalized (Sister Dorothea is one of her nurses), for she sees Matern's dog in its true light as the hound of hell. And she sees both her presumptive fathers, Matern and Sawatzki, along with seven other SA men beating out Eddi Amsel's teeth.

Meanwhile, Matern has located his father the miller, who has survived the trek west—Matern's mother and aunt drown when their ship hits a mine—with his sack of flour and its mealworms still intact. When the sack-toting miller is suspected of being a black marketeer, an official of the occupation forces, Mr. Brooks, intervenes on his behalf and ensconces him in a remodeled old mill.

Here, as a kind of negative counterpole to the enlightening effect of the magical eyeglasses, the miller opens an occult consulting firm based on the soothsaying powers of his worms. Those who follow the worms' effective but essentially amoral advice are shown loopholes in the attempts by the occupation forces to break up wartime cartels and establish a responsible press. They soon become the powerful leaders of postwar Germany, architects of the economic miracle, of reindustrialization and of rearmament. Ludwig Erhard, minister of finance under Adenauer and his successor as chancellor, receives his very own mealworm to swallow. Axel Springer is advised to found his reactionary yellow tabloid *Bildzeitung*, with which three million reading illiterates will henceforth have their breakfast.

The first choice of the worms for chancellor is Hans Globke, one of the lawyers who formulated the infamous Nuremberg race laws but whom the worms characterize as a quiet resistance fighter. When Konrad Adenauer is elected instead, the worms work behind the scenes and manage to salvage a partial victory by having Globke appointed as his assistant.

"Don't listen to the worm, the worm is wormy!," the Social Democratic opposition warns (Hj 501). Though it costs them votes, they refuse to go along with what they call such medieval, devilish hocus-pocus, and they recommend a worm cure for the entire capitalist system.

The younger Matern takes a job managing the prospering mill, its parking lot for limousines, its offices, its telephone switchboard, and its bar where clients meet after hours to discuss affairs. Here, over gin and whiskey at midnight, Matern, who was red, wore brown, became black, and has returned to red, advances his Marxist ideas, thus synchronizing Communistic worm myths with capitalistic ones. His friends from big business agree with him since they were all on the left themselves once, they say.

Even when Matern has leaflets printed with a leftist text on the left side of the page, his capitalist clients use the blank right side to make notes about dividends, investments, tax credits, industrial capacities, and cartel arrangements. This provides a strik-

ing symbolic anticipation, we read, of the coexis-
tence, the essential moral equality, of East and West,
left and right.

Though tight security for the mill is provided by
Western intelligence agencies intent on preventing
the East Germans from obtaining useful worm wisdom, one case of attempted arson does occur at the
time of Stalin's death. And on the day preceding the
workers' uprising in East Berlin on June 17, 1953,
the miller Matern—along with his sack—is kidnap-
ped, presumably by Communists. West German leaders are frightened. For them the miller's departure is
more serious even than that of Bismark, portrayed in
the famous English caricature of the time: now the
pilot is leaving the *sinking* ship.

But no calamity occurs. The German ship of state
holds the course set by the worms and sails on into
further prosperity. The worms are soon forgotten and
the innate diligence of the German people, who, with
God's grace, rise like the phoenix from the ashes, is
given credit for the miraculous recovery.

Upon the departure of his father Matern is left un-
employed once again. He returns to the Sawatzkis in
Düsseldorf—Oskar is now playing at the Onion Cellar, they tell him—and he has dinner at the Morgue,
where he sees the teeth pudding. He tries to play
Faustball with his old athletic club, but without the
intelligent team leader Amsel, and with his legendary physical prowess badly undermined by debauch
and dissipation, the now impotent Matern must become a referee. Then he becomes a coach to younger
players with whom he also shares his hypocritical
views on history and politics, placing the usual

blame on everyone but himself. Of course, history repeats itself: Matern is thrown out of the athletic club
for the second time for preaching Communist propaganda.

In his endless campaign to take revenge Matern
learns the whereabouts of Rolf Zander, former dra-
maturge of the theater in Schwerin who had once
fired him for drunkenness and for spouting slogans.
When Matern attempts to avenge himself on Zander,
now an important cultural editor at West German
Radio in Cologne, by poisoning the trees surrounding
Zander's villa, a strong downpour washes away the
herbicide, and Zander welcomes Matern with open
arms, offering him an acting job at the radio station.
Matern's frightening voice lends itself to such roles
as Schiller's robber chieftain, a fairy-tale wolf, a rab-
ble rouser, a Judas, an SS man, a slave driver, and a
blasphemer. Like "Oskarism," a new term, "Mater-
noid," is coined to describe the fear of the children
who hear him.

It also happens in this thickening plot, clearly
stage-managed by Brauxel, that Harry Liebenau
works for West German Radio. Though Matern is
suspicious of him for the same reasons Brauxel hires
him (he has a filing cabinet memory of what happened in Danzig, for example, as well as a penchant
for making connections and for getting to the bottom
of things), Matern agrees to speak the leading role in
one of Liebenau's projects called "A Public Discussion."

This surrealistic discussion turns out to be an ex-
posé of Matern's life in the form of an ancient Greek
drama, set in a replica of the Gutenberg monument

96

from Danzig. It is complete with a speech chorus of thirty-two young participants, including Walli Sawatzki, who has her magic eyeglasses at hand to prevent Matern from lying. This dramatic last judgment ascertains that though Matern claims to be an animal lover, he has a record of killing animals: a dog, countless crows, a canary. Though he claims to have been Eddi Amsel's protecter and a philo-Semite, he beat Eddi and called him "Itzig." Though he claims to be an antifascist, born on April 19, he is actually the heir to Hitler's wolfish dog, was born on Hitler's birthday, April 20, and gnashes his teeth as Hitler did, establishing his total ontological identity with this, the greatest criminal of all time.

At the first reading of the script a horrified Matern flees Cologne for East Germany, leaving the aging Pluto behind. But as the train speeds along through West and then East Germany, he thinks he sees Eddi's military scarecrows mobilizing alongside the tracks and then racing the train in relays through the countryside. And he sees a black dog with them, growing younger as it races eastward, and backward, toward its violent origins.

Though he annoys even the East Germans, driving them out of his compartment with his glowing praise of the communist system, the pragmatic Matern does decide to stop in West Berlin to purchase a few items and change his money at a better rate before proceeding to East Berlin. At the station he is met by the rejuvenated Pluto and Goldmäulchen, who claims the dog found him and led him to Matern.

They go out for drinks together—Goldmäulchen drinks only hot lemonade for the chronic hoarseness

97

caused by his sojourn inside the snowman—and spend the evening hopping from bar to bar and telling stories. Goldmäulchen tells about two blood brothers, one of whom threw a pocketknife into a river. Then he produces a rusty knife which he has had dredged up and presents it to Matern.

They arrive at Chez Jenny, a bar in an old wooden barrack, the proprietress of which is, of course, Jenny Angustri-Brunies. Jenny prepares the hot lemonade for the visionary Goldmäulchen according to an old Gypsy recipe, by adding a pinch of mnemonic mica chips. As Matern recounts tales of his ancestor, the cosmic arsonist Materna, the chain-smoker Goldmäulchen throws his butts on the wooden floor and the bar itself turns into a fiery hell with Matern, its hellish guest, roaring Communist slogans through the flames.

After they leave the bar and walk Jenny home, the men stop on a bridge over a canal. Again Matern throws the knife into the water, but Goldmäulchen assures him the canal can easily be drained and the knife reclaimed. In his anger Matern screams "Itzig!" and then, exhausted and inebriated, worn down finally by Goldmäulchen's perseverance, he collapses. Goldmäulchen hails a cab, and they depart for a final confrontation at the potash mine near Hannover.

Here in the mine, which reminds Matern, and the reader, of Dante's *Inferno*, Matern finds his father employed as the gate keeper. The appropriateness of the name for Amsel's sketchbook, *Pandämonium*, is fully realized. Even the hardened, violent Matern is horrified by the bedlam, by the countless varieties and psychotic activities of the most bizarre scarecrows. He is shocked by the hellish laughter, the teeth gnashing, the scarecrow sporting events, the religious and military services, the scarecrow emotions, hate, anger, revenge, by the scarecrow priapism and the scarecrow impotence. "This is hell!" Matern says over and over again (Hj 673). Not so, Brauxel maintains, "Orcus is above ground," (Hj 681), and again he reminds Matern of Brauxel's other motto: The scarecrow is created in the image of man.

As the novel ends, Matern and Brauxel come up from the underworld, leaving Pluto below, and take a bath, something like a washing and a rebirth, but each in his own way. Will Matern be purged of his essential evil? Grass does not say. "We are both naked . . . each one bathes alone [or for himself]" (Hj 682).

Dog Years, for all its complexities, is at bottom simple and clear: in Amsel/Brauxel, Grass has created a visionary artist who, like himself, re-creates in all manifestations of his art the hidden, and hideous, essence of evil. His scarecrows are copies of the *Schweinehunde* he sees above ground.

And though Amsel's works, like the works of Günter Grass himself, shock, horrify, and elicit criticism and abuse (there is evidence, for example, that details not only of the sales patterns but of the legal complaints involving Brauxel's magic eyeglasses are identical to those involving *The Tin Drum* and *Cat and Mouse*[1]) they are shocking and horrifying because they reveal real, not imaginary abuses. Eddi does not build "against" anyone, we are constantly reminded; he intends to demonstrate to "a dangerously productive environment, some productivity of his own" (Hj 218).

Thus his fiery atomic gods are Old Prussian artistic models of actual atomic weapons, such as ballistic missiles to which men in the upper world also attach the names of gods: Poseidon, Atlas, Nike. His scarecrows populate the entire globe from Africa to the atomic testing grounds of Nevada.

And yet, as the day of nuclear wrath draws ever nearer and as Brauxel, consulting the stars, prepares to have to make a mimetic mirroring of the event in the Great Cuckoo Bird, the artist focuses his visionary optical powers primarily on Germany. It is the primary heir of the hound of hell, and the confrontation site par excellence for the global powers. His secondary focus is on the troubled Middle East and the Jews, the blood brothers to the Germans, indelibly marked and fated by their common past to write together the history of the future. On the bridge in Berlin the half-Jew Amsel says to the German Matern, "But among all peoples, which exist as scarecrow arsenals, it is first and foremost the German people, which, even more than the Jewish people, has within it all the right stuff to one day bestow upon the world the archscarecrow" (Hj 646f).

NOTE

1. See Alan Frank Keele, *The Apocalyptic Vision* (Washington: *studia humanitatis*, 1983), 22–27.

CHAPTER FOUR

Local Anaesthetic
örtlich betäubt

AFTER *DOG YEARS* APPEARED, THERE WERE, LIKE THE
ballet "The Scarecrows," artistic offshoots from the
project. A play entitled "Goldmäulchen" was produced in Munich in 1963, and the "Public Discussion" from Book 3 was broadcast by Hessian Radio.

In 1965, the year his son Bruno was born, Grass
was awarded an honorary doctorate from Kenyon
College. He also received the prestigious Georg Büch-
ner Prize from the German Academy for Language
and Literature in Darmstadt. That year Grass made
over fifty appearances on a campaign tour for the Social Democratic Party, during which a firebomb was
thrown at his front door. And he wrote the drama
*Die Plebejer proben den Aufstand (The Plebeians Re-
hearse the Uprising,)* produced in Berlin in 1966.

In 1966 he traveled to the meeting of the Group 47
in Princeton as well as to Czechoslovakia and to
Hungary. He was involved in the campaign during
the state elections in Bavaria. *Cat and Mouse* was
filmed. Grass began, with Elisabeth Borchers and
Klaus Roehler, to edit an ongoing "looseleaf" poetry
series for the Luchterhand publishing firm called
Luchterhand Loseblatt Lyrik. He continued to write
and deliver political messages, only a small portion

101

of which, by 1968, had filled a book: *Über das Selbst-verständliche, Reden, Aufsätze, offene Briefe, Kommentare* (On the Self-evident, Speeches, Essays, Open Letters, Commentaries).

He began to write what would become (from 1970 to 1972) a regular column for *Die Süddeutsche Zeitung* in Munich. A volume of poetry and drawings entitled *Ausgefragt* (Thoroughly Interrogated) appeared in 1967. In that year Grass campaigned in Schleswig-Holstein and in Berlin. He traveled to Israel. He carried on an extensive correspondence with the Czech writer Pavel Kohout, published in 1968 as *Briefe über die Grenze: Versuch eines Ost-West-Dialogs* (Letters Across the Border: An Attempt at an East-West Dialogue). And he won the Carl von Ossietzky Medal (named in honor of the Nobel Prize–winning pacifist journalist persecuted by the Nazis).

The next year he won the Fontane Prize, the annual literary award of the city of West Berlin named after the nineteenth-century author Theodor Fontane. He gave a major speech at the Social Democratic Party Convention in Nuremberg. All during these busy years the indefatigable Grass was preparing a new literary work, the novel *Local Anaesthetic* (1969) and a dramatic version of the same material entitled *Davor* (literally: Before That, translated as *Max: A Play*).

Not a few readers were perplexed by Grass's new work, a tale ostensibly told this time not by a mental but a dental patient. With the narrator's mouth anaesthetized and blocked open, *Local Anaesthetic* is, as the first sentence informs us, a tale without sound. Hence it is in reality an interior monologue, a

102

reversal of a normal dentist's conversation. It is a stream of consciousness projected onto the office television screen with whose advertisements and other regular features the narrator freely associates.

Fading from one scene, from one imagined discussion to another, this complex verbal-video collage gradually introduces the reader or the viewer to the fragmented mind, life, and times of one Eberhard Starusch, a forty-year-old secondary teacher of German and history living in Berlin during the turbulent era of the war in Vietnam. Structurally it seemed a new departure to readers who had forgotten how Grass had already blended in boldly experimental ways epic and dramatic elements in the Danzig trilogy: the theater of the absurd staged at the bunkers in Normandy, for example, or the public discussion and the scarecrow ballet.

Appearing to deal almost entirely with contemporary problems, the contents of the work also did not seem to fit the pattern of the books of the Danzig trilogy, with their heavy emphasis on the past. And yet *Local Anaesthetic* is a most logical extension of Grass's earlier work. It has its roots in prewar and wartime Danzig, in the juvenile milieu of Oskar and the Duster Gang. And, like the previous works, it follows these characters and the legacy of that violent period into the postwar present, reemphasizing the central thrust of the trilogy: that the present is the heir of the black cooks and the black dogs of the past and must now and forever command our attention.

The violent attitudes and bizarre behavior of the unreliable first-person narrator, Eberhard Starusch, for example, are only partially due to the mildly psychedelic side effects of his anaesthetic. They make better sense when one discovers he is identical with the boy nicknamed Störtebeker, erstwhile leader of the Duster Gang, disciple of Oskar Matzerath and of Walter Matern from the Danzig trilogy.

Now Old Hardy, as the students call him, experiences something like *déjà vu*. He and they, the same age he was under Nazism, are confronted with a not-so-vaguely familiar set of problems. An ex-Nazi, Kurt Georg Kiesinger, is federal chancellor of West Germany. Germany has rearmed to the teeth. Its major ally, the United States, is now engaged in an unjust, genocidal war of aggression in Southeast Asia. Surely there is something rotten in this state of affairs.

And there is literally something rotten in Starusch, the symbolic personification of this state: he requires extensive dental work. Grass had used teeth and tooth decay before as tangible symbols of less tangible psychological and social conditions. Pilenz is suffering from a toothache on the first pages of *Cat and Mouse*. Matern, like Hitler a tooth-gnasher, knocks out all thirty-two of Amsel's perfect white teeth and is later served teeth pudding arranged for by Goldmäulchen.

And in the poem "Kleine Aufforderung zum grossen Mundaufmachen—oder der Wasserspeier spricht" (A Little Call for a Big Mouthopening—or the Gargoyle Speaks) from *Gleisdreieck*, Grass associates the putrescence that has lived on "behind the toothpaste" with those horrible gold teeth "that we broke out of and harvested from the dead" (GG 142). To rid

104

ourselves of it we must open our mouths, that is, speak out. In *Local Anaesthetic*, Starusch's tartar is described as his calcified hate. This, together with his confused thinking, especially about the past, causes putrescent pockets of bacteria to form.

In addition, Starusch has a striking innate under-bite, a "Mussolini chin" as it is called, a visible symbol of his tendency to fascist brutality. This tendency also emerges when the teacher regales his seventeen-year-old students with romantic tales about his glory days as the leader of the anarchic Duster Gang. He boasts it was indeed his group that set fire to the submarine tender. He tells them about other, historical, teen-aged wartime gangs such as the Edelweiss Pirates in Cologne, upon which the Dusters are modeled, all the while characterizing his group as resistance fighters: "We put up real resistance" (öb 16).

However, his prize pupil, Phillip Scherbaum, decides to be a resistance fighter himself against what he sees as modern parallels to the wartime period. Phillip conceives a plan to soak his beloved dachshund Max with gasoline and immolate him in front of the fashionable Cafe Kempinski on the Kurfürstendamm as a protest against the use of napalm in Vietnam. A horrified Starusch attempts to convince him to give up this juvenile anarchism and to become the editor of the school paper.

Scherbaum's radical girlfriend is Vero Lewand, a reincarnation of the seductive Tulla Prokriefke, that dog-killing Black Cook figure from the Danzig trilogy. Vero, a disciple of Che Guevara and of Mao (Mao's calls for sacrifice are here compared with

105

those of Hitler), urges him to kill the dog. She tries
to seduce and then blackmail Starusch in order to
prevent him from interfering.

Vero is the juvenile alter ego—in this symmetrical
cast—of Irmgard Seifert, Starusch's female counterpart and fiancée. Seifert is also a teacher at the
school; in 1945, as a zealous seventeen-year-old Nazi,
she had written glowing hymns to the Führer and
had trained children in the use of antitank weapons.
She had also denounced a farmer to the police for re-
fusing to allow a tank trap to be dug in his field. Yet
until she finds some of her old wartime letters, she
likewise firmly believes she was, and always char-
acterizes herself as, a bold resistance fighter.

Known to her present students as the Archangel
because her speeches resemble a flaming sword,
Seifert is still a religious mystic. She is inclined to
see in the brave young Scherbaum a political savior,
a kind of Great Mahlke struck by the Holy Ghost
and glowing with light, who will purify a corrupt
society by fire. (Ironically, however, her practical
advice to her worried colleague and fiancé is that he
should denounce Scherbaum to the police.)

The dentist, of course, says he is opposed to the immolation. As a rational man of science and a student
of the Stoic philosophers, even though he radically
removes Starusch's symbolic tartar, he professes to
believe the treatment of dental—and societal—decay
should be prophylactic rather than radical. He maintains systems should be reformed rather than eliminated. He even proposes a system of universal health
care which would solve all the world's problems. Yet
when Starusch reverts to his innate impulses to solve

the world's problems radically—when he projects, for
example, onto the television screen metaphoric bull-
dozers which would clear the world of its corrupt systems—the dentist threatens him with pain if he does
not recant.

But Starusch's violent streak runs even deeper
than that of the dentist. A good portion of his narrative concerns his former fiancée Linde Krings and
her other incarnations, whom a jealous Starusch
murders—at first verbally—and then remurders in a
lengthy series of bizarre fantasies.

Eventually the narrative returns to the central
question of the novel: the immolation of the dog. Despite his ambivalence about the matter Starusch
knows he may get in trouble himself if his student
goes through with it. So the teacher goes to great
lengths to persuade him to desist. He makes one last
pedagogical attempt to deter Phillip by rehearsing
with him the fate of a seventeen-year-old student
named Bartholdy who, in 1797, received a life sentence for attempting to import the French Revolution
into Prussian Danzig. Then Starusch—deep down the
frustrated and impotent middle-aged liberal would
like to relive through Phillip's deed his own exciting
youth—finally blurts out: "Do it, please, do it (öb 274).

The solution comes from an unexpected quarter. It
comes from history, not from the French Revolution,
but from the very era of the Duster Gang, from the
very generation of the impotent history teacher himself. On his own, in a trade union newspaper, seventeen-year-old Phillip Scherbaum has discovered a
historical account of seventeen-year-old Helmuth
Hübener. Hübener, the leader of a nonviolent resis-

tance group, composed and distributed antifascist leaflets and was beheaded by the Nazis in 1942. Hübener's photo now hangs on Phillip's wall, even as Che Guevara's hangs on Vero's.

Phillip lectures his history teacher on Hübener's activities: "He didn't waste his time demolishing churches and the like. Not a trace of Early Anarchism. He wasn't an amateur like your Bartholdy either. He could take stenography, and he even knew Morse code" (öb 281).

Starusch vaguely recalls reading something about Hübener once and is stricken with professional guilt. The teacher now also realizes why with his gang leader's past he could never have been Phillip's model.

Scherbaum renames the school paper "Morsezeichen" (Morse Code), and writes an inaugural article dealing with Helmuth Hübener's resistance group, comparing the activities of Chancellor Kiesinger and Hübener in the year 1942. He has given up the idea of burning Max and is having his teeth fixed.

But what of Starusch? Will the teacher ever learn? Will he ever find a nonviolent model like Helmuth Hübener? Will he be forever hagridden and hounded by black cooks and black dogs? As it ends, the novel leaps ahead by two years. Vero Lewand has married a Canadian linguist, and Phillip Scherbaum is studying medicine.

For his part, Starusch develops another serious abscess, a sure sign of wildly growing hate complexes, as the dentist earlier explained, for Starusch is one of those archetypical German "Abgewiesene

Zukurzgekommene Versager" (rejects also-rans duds)
like Adolf Hitler. "They leaf through pulp magazines
with their toothache locally anaesthetized. They invent enemies and stories in which their invented
enemies are liquidated. They paint the word *Revolution* on their shaving mirrors, "und wollen ausmer-
zen abschaffen stillmachen" (and want to eradicate
exterminate eliminate [öb 97]). For them violence is
ersatz virility, and by the creation of fictions they
project their own impotence onto the rest of the
world so they can have a valid reason to destroy it.
They desire the Nietzschean reevaluation of all
values and want to go beyond human beings (öb 144)
yet avoid the appearance of an old-fashioned appeal
for the Socialist Man. They measure with absolute
measures. They yawn at others' attempts to make
useful improvements. They wish to cut through knots
with sword strokes. They lust after the most splendid
downfall of civilization. They flee from their problems into doctrines of salvation, and they promise a
millennial paradise after a relatively short period of
violence.

Though they brought Hitler to power, in their
selective memories they imagine themselves to have
been resistance fighters. Now they imagine themselves—and appear on the surface—to be antifascists,
liberals, and democrats. Deep down, however, they
are still unreconstructed fascists awaiting any opportunity for recrudescence. This is revealed in their
speech—"I'll kill you" (öb 134)—in their vulgar and
violent reading and viewing preferences, and in their
sanguinary fantasies. Walter Matern was such an
antihero and so is Starusch.

But Phillip Scherbaum is Grass's new, positive, contemporary hero. Standing on the shoulders of dwarves like Oskar, his visual acuity enhanced by the eyeglasses of Eddi Amsel, this young hero looks the present clearly in the face. He does not mythologize; he does not seek to be or to follow a messiah; and he rejects easy, violent solutions, patterning his actions after Helmuth Hübener, who patiently sought to educate and enlighten the German people about Hitler. His heraldic animal could be the snail, a symbol of slow, patient progress.

From the Diary of a Snail (Aus dem Tagebuch einer Schnecke)

THE SNAIL IS ALSO GRASS'S SYMBOL FOR HIMSELF AND for his political models. In 1969 Grass participated in a campaign tour to found grass-roots voter initiatives for the Social Democratic Party throughout the Federal Republic. This involved making almost two hundred appearances and a hundred speeches. Accounts of this campaign gradually accumulate in Grass's *Sudelbuch* (scribble book) and form the basis for *From the Diary of a Snail*. This work contains his notes on a speech about Albrecht Dürer's engraving "Melencholia I." (The city of Nuremberg invited Grass to give this speech in 1971 for the celebration of the five hundredth anniversary of Dürer's birth.) It documents Grass's involvement with political figures such as Herbert Wehner, chairman of the Social Democratic Party, and Egon Bahr, Willy Brandt's closest political confidant. It treats the archetypical snail, Willy Brandt himself, and calls him the heir of the prototypical snail, August Bebel, the founder of the Social Democratic Party. It tells of trips to Yugoslavia, France, Israel, and Czechoslovakia. It recounts Grass's participation in a Lutheran Church conference in Stuttgart. And it documents the successful election in September 1969, when Willy Brandt was finally elected federal Chancellor.

As always in Grass there is a fictive, historical background, a tale set in prewar and wartime Danzig. The protagonist of this tale, whose experiences are based loosely on those of the literary critic Marcel Reich-Ranicki, is Hermann Ott. He is nicknamed Zweifel (Doubt) because of his disposition to question commonly accepted "facts." Through Ott, who is a teacher at a Jewish school, Grass relates the fate of the Jews in Danzig. Also through Ott, a collector of snails, Grass displays his own encyclopedic knowledge of gastropoda as he did in previous works with such subjects as dentistry, mining, and stone carving.

Through Lisbeth Stomma, a woman suffering from severe depression whom Ott later marries (after which he himself becomes a melancholic), Grass links his ruminations on "Melencholia I." He portrays his own political efforts as an attempt to inject a shade of gray into the "black" thinking of voters for the Christian parties, as an attempt to cure the body politic of its excess of black gall (*melan-choly*).

Even though much of the diary is fictional and has close ties to the earlier novels, especially to *Local Anaesthetic*, Grass steps out from behind his fictional masks more often here, providing the reader with the most private view of the author and his family to date. But even when Grass discusses his love for cooking and his preference for unusual visceral dishes such as cow's stomach, calves' kidneys on celery, chopped lung, and beef heart stuffed with plums, he makes a political point: none of the ideologies he has been fed, with their articles of faith and their conjurations of utopian goals, are palatable.

Marxism, cooked into a thick goo or, as usual, watered down, reminds him only of an egalitarian barley soup lacking all herbs and spices. For Grass is an epicure who would be happier, he says, if all those who wish to teach him how to live also enjoyed life: "The betterment of the world should not remain entrusted to dyspeptic soreheads" (AT 91).

Grass, we learn, is a revisionist, a follower of Eduard Bernstein and of Arthur Schopenhauer, who taught him to look at the world before forming an opinion. Consequently, he is an opponent of Georg Wilhelm Friedrich Hegel, who did things the other way around. Grass also dislikes bigoted Catholics, orthodox atheists, and those who wish to straighten out bananas in the interest of humankind. He likes old, broken people, skat, buttermilk and radishes, his children's antics, and the sight of his wife altering a new dress. His favorite flower is the light-gray *Skepsis* (skepticism). Of course his favorite color is gray— hence his love for pencil drawings—because "gray proves that there is no black anywhere" (AT 87).

From the Diary of a Snail is addressed to Grass's children as an object lesson in history and its application to modern problems. He is an improved Starusch. They are all potential Scherbaums. Their angry words over spilled water at the dinner table— "Sau!" (pig!), "Obersau!" (chief pig! [AT 14]—can become the catalyst for lectures on the intellectual and

113

verbal origins of violence and wars: "Ideas herald violence; it is possible to resist them. Therefore resistance must begin before ideas attain violence" (AT 173).

The mention of Biafra on television can become a catalyst for lectures on the search for scapegoats, on verbal stereotyping and the genesis of genocide: "That's how it begins, children: The Jews are. The migrant workers want . . . The Blacks. The Leftists". The text may change on these signposts, Grass says, but the verbal signs themselves always point toward the same violent destination: "annihilate expose convert destroy abolish pacify liquidate reeducate isolate eradicate" (AT 20).

This stainless-steel language, these doubly hardened cutting words, are well known to Grass's snail, he says, which he introduces at the beginning of the book. Here he tells Franz, Raoul, Laura, and Bruno that when he observed the election of Gustav Heinemann as federal president in March 1969, their father narrowed his eyes into "seeing slits" (in the manner of Eddi Amsel) and saw a giant snail creep slowly through the hall: "That I can do, children, clearly imagine something" (AT 8).

She hesitated, Grass perceived (in German snails are feminine, a detail whose importance is revealed more clearly in *The Flounder*), with her feelers out, not wishing to arrive at her goal, not wishing to win. But when Grass promises her a new goal, when he baits her with food, slices of the future, she crosses this finish line—Heinemann wins by a narrow margin—and creeps forward toward the victory of Willy Brandt in September.

114

This snail, Grass's symbol for the progress of democracy, freedom, and reason, "wins just barely and seldom. She . . . draws her rapidly drying glide track in the historical landscape, over documents and borders, between building sites and ruins, through drafty intellectual constructs, away from nicely placed theories, alongside retreats and past revolutions stuck in the sand" (AT 9).

The rigors of the election campaign, the *Wahlkampf* (four-year-old Bruno, confused by the homophone *Walkampf*, imagines his father off harpooning whales), include daily confrontations with radical young people. Their language is characterized by Grass as "the lower-case language of the destroying angel—tough totally completely pure drastic." These are people who are dedicated "to the unconditionally irreconcilable, unqualifiedly unswerving, irresistible merciless rectification of the world," Grass says (AT 20). Then he invokes the metaphor "Freisler finger on Lenin's hand," a reference to the infamous Nazi hanging judge Roland Freisler, chief of the bloody People's Tribunal. (Before returning to Germany and becoming a Nazi, Freisler had been, as an ethnic German living in the Soviet Union, a commissar of the Ukraine under Lenin.) The implication is that the totalitarianisms of the left and of the right employ the same absolutist rhetoric and are essentially identical: the language of these young revolutionaries is identical with that of fascists. Which crusade will enlist them?

As if to answer his own question, Grass shifts to March 1933, to Danzig, where young Nazis have been harassing Jewish students, making it impossible for them to continue their studies. Shifting back to the present, he continues to describe the modern analogue, Marxist students, with their misplaced religious fervor (replete with echoes from the Danzig novels): "Everywhere they want to raise the level of consciousness of other people before they raise their own: too-well housed sons who rave about the proletariat like it was a manifestation of the Virgin Mary . . . lately, professional gladiators for God, who pour the blood of Christ into Hegel-shaped bottles" (AT 52).

Grass encounters more of these young people in Stuttgart at the Lutheran Church conference (where he reads to them about Scherbaum wanting to burn his dachshund): "Many barefooted, and, now that it's too late, early-Christian young people hunger for a new myth, want to believe in something, have a paradisiacal look in their eye and will hop over the barrier of reason" (AT 191).

And then came August, Grass says, employing once again his familiar technique of associative juxtapositioning. Actually there are at least two Augusts—the elder August, a former SS man, and a parallel young "August," one of the gladiators for God, a messiah figure surrounded by Magdalenes. Both Augusts are really identical since both are timeless exemplars, both "witnesses for the absolute," (AT 192) both seeking the warmth of a conspiratorial community, the SS in the case of the elder, the coming revolution in the case of the younger.

The elder August, a member of the Free Christian Church, the postwar heir to the (Nazi) Church of German Christians, who also happens to be a drug-

gist, takes the microphone, salutes his old SS comrades, and drains a flask of potassium cyanide. Grass
again discourses on the similarity of cyanide and
almonds as he had in *The Tin Drum*. Eventually he
visits August's family, hoping to understand his
motivation: what Black Cook caused his state of
melancholy, his black depression.

August's story becomes one of the major subplots of
this complex and skillfully crafted diary. As the
Apollo 11 astronauts walk on the moon, the Grass
family receives telephoned death threats. They take
a short vacation near the concrete bunkers in Brit-
tany and a trip to Israel, where Grass interviews sur-
viving Jews from Danzig (and on November 9–10,
thirty-three years after the Crystal Night, is heckled
by young right-wing Jews crying that Germans are
murderers). They travel to Czechoslovakia to visit
their friends Franticek, Olga, and Vladimir. This
occasion permits Grass to warn his children about
the easy solutions promised by Communism. He comments on the tragic irony that whereas in 1938 it
had been Adolf Hitler, in 1968 it was Leonid Brezh-
nev who sent German troops, dressed in Prussian-cut
uniforms, across the border once again to occupy
Czechoslovakia.

Meanwhile, Hermann Ott and the Jews of Danzig
confront the inexorable rise of Nazism. It is not long
before his oracular snails reveal to the visionary Ott,
who is by no means a Zionist, and is in fact not a
Jew at all but a Mennonite, that he should nonetheless urge his Jewish friends to think about emigra-
tion. Some of these friends, however, like the orthodox Isaak Laban, are also chauvinistic German

nationalists, veterans of World War I, who at first refuse to believe any harm can come to them.

But the violence escalates. The Jewish merchants like Laban the greengrocer are driven away from the marketplace into a separate ghetto and their customers harassed. The synagogues are burned even though uniformed Jewish veterans like Laban manage to guard one of them and prevent its destruction. Even Laban begins to realize he must leave, that he must "pay a visit to Semmelmann," as the saying goes, a cryptic statement that he must buy some suitcases at Semmelmann's luggage shop. But it is SA men who first pay Herr Semmelmann a visit, breaking up his establishment and giving him a fatal beating with his own tools.

The Jewish school closes and Ott meets with his remaining students in his home, which then becomes the object of a police search. He helps pack the Torah and other sacred items from the synagogue for shipment to the Jewish Museum in New York. Small groups of children are sent to England, many of them never to see their parents again.

A concentration camp is established at Stutthof, and the Jews are told to give up their homes. Many commit suicide, many more are taken to Stutthof, and others are forced into a ghetto. Some attempt to flee to the south, but they are caught by German troops near the Carpathians, shot, and buried in mass graves in the forest. A group of fifty do manage to reach Vienna by train, but they are interned in Yugoslavia along with a thousand others, and with three exceptions all are later murdered by German commandos.

After he is badly beaten by a gang of Hitler Youth and brutally interrogated by the police about his association with the Jews, Ott begins to think about escaping from Danzig himself. He packs his suitcase and rides out of Danzig on his bicycle. In Karthaus he stops to have a flat tire repaired. He negotiates with the Kashubian bicycle dealer Anton Stomma for a place to hide in a cellar storage room for the duration, a year or so, as he believes, until the Germans "have conquered themselves to bits" (AT 150).

The widower Stomma has a daughter, Lisbeth, whose Polish lover Roman and her three-year-old child Hannes were killed at the beginning of the war. Lisbeth suffers from aphasia due to severe melancholy. She hardly speaks to the living but spends all her time at the cemetery, where she converses with the dead as if they were all still alive, a practice prompting the neighbors to consider her insane.

One day Ott discovers a snail which has been brought into the cellar along with some potatoes. Seeing his delight at the sight of it, Lisbeth begins to bring him more snails, and soon Ott is fighting against boredom and impatience by staging snail races—to him a form of microcosmic augury assuring the slow but certain victory of the Allied forces. And then in August 1944, as the German armies are indeed in retreat, Lisbeth finds a purple-red snail on her son's grave, which even the specialist Ott cannot identify. It has the peculiar ability when placed on her skin to heal Lisbeth of her aphasia. She begins to relate freely her conversations with Hannes and with the other dead.

119

Gradually the snail draws out of Lisbeth all her melancholy, her black bile, itself becoming darker and darker in the process. She begins to sing again, she goes less and less often to the cemetery, and she becomes a passionate lover. As if her devil, all the evil and blackness of her times, had been drawn into the snail, Lisbeth now begins to curse it and spit on it. Eventually, as the German armies are finally crushed, she crushes the blue-black snail beneath her foot—"Nailing the snail to the cross," as Grass puts it (AT 314).

With a note on his high hopes for the new German comprehensive school which he believes will increase the snail-like character of his children, the diary proper ends. But Grass's speech at the Dürer conference entitled "On Standing Still in Progress, Variations on Albrecht Dürer's etching 'Melencholia I'", is appended to the book and forms a kind of final chapter.

This speech is a brilliant tour de force, encompassing not only a summary of his engagement with political problems, of the writing of his snail diary, and of the entire narrative fabric of the diary itself, but an imaginative, often fantastic exploration of the psychosocial roots of depression in suburban housewives and assembly-line workers. It is an analysis of the dark side of euphoric utopian expectations whether in the planned societies of the East Bloc or in the artificial "say-cheese!" smiles of consumerism and "the American way of life." It is an erudite inventory of modern malaises and their historical roots in Dürer's time, at the end of the Middle Ages and the beginning of the new age of "progress."

But it also guardedly hints at a prescription for the condition, for the exorcism of the Black Cook. Follow the snail. Don't count on it making utopian leaps. Don't expect too much progress too easily, but don't give up. Only those who know and appreciate what it is like to have progress stand still, who have given up several times over, who have experienced the dark side of utopia, can measure true progress.

From the Diary of a Snail was written almost entirely during 1969. Only a few episodes at the end date from the years 1970 and 1971, an indication that Grass delayed its publication, timing it to coincide with the next federal elections, held in 1972. Thus, a literary account of one election campaign becomes a political tool released just in time to aid in the next. Grass could not have made his point more clearly: that he believes politics and art *can* coexist.

As might be expected, Grass again made a large number of appearances, about 130 in all, during the successful campaign of 1972 which strengthened the mandate for Willy Brandt and his initiatives, including *Ostpolitik* and détente. Grass's relationship to Willy Brandt remained strong. He accompanied Brandt on his historic trips to East Germany and to Poland (1970), where Brandt knelt in Warsaw before the memorial to the victims of Nazism, as well as to Israel and to the United States (1973).

Yet Grass was not afraid to criticize Brandt and the Social Democrats as he had earlier when they agreed to form the Grand Coalition with ex-Nazi Kiesinger as chancellor. Grass has never been one to withhold his opinion out of fear he might be disliked. When Grass, like Amsel, believes he perceives present parallels to past errors, even when these may be only aesthetic, too subtle to convince many others, and even when it may offend his friends and nearest allies, he speaks out.

A case in point occurred in 1972, when Heinar Kipphardt produced in Munich a play by Wolf Biermann on the subject of dragon slaying. The printed program, for which Kipphardt was officially responsible (but which was never publicly released), showed the pictures of prominent civic leaders. For Grass, as for some of those depicted in the program, the implication was clear: here were dragons that needed to be slain.

In his regular column in the *Süddeutsche Zeitung*, Grass sternly lectured Kipphardt. The ensuing imbroglio resulted in Kipphardt being replaced as director, but it also made Grass a number of enemies on the left, especially among the literati and intelligentsia, many of whom had always assumed that Grass, the stalwart antifascist and enemy of the extreme right, was naturally their ally.

Though he now had a whole new category of enemies on the left, the passage of time has demonstrated that Grass's vision was acute, his fears about the revival of something like a Duster Gang of the left well founded. German terrorist groups like the one under Andreas Baader and Ulrike Meinhof began to arise just at this time in just those quarters Grass predicted. They arose among disenchanted utopian leftists, many of them women, who were impatient with the snail's pace of progress, who wanted something to believe in, who wanted a new religion of revolution, and who felt that humanistic ends could justify violent means.

For equating the extreme left with the extreme right, Grass also appears, in hindsight, to have been less politically naive than he has been portrayed. Modern international terrorism, unified by violence, flows as easily across traditional political categories as it does across geographical borders.

Other, often very respected antifascist authors such as Nobel laureate Heinrich Böll were at this time flirting with the allure of violent revolution. Böll's heros, particularly his female heroes (at least one of which, Katharina Blum, appears directly based on the figure of Ulrike Meinhof), are especially prone to solve their problems with firearms. But Grass makes the antifascist Walter Matern the heir of Hitler's dog. He analyses the frustration of mid-life intellectuals in the character of Eberhard Starusch. He addresses the need to find a new messiah and join a crusade in the characters of Pilenz, Vero Lewand, and Irmgard Seifert. He suggests the alternative nonviolent model of Helmuth Hübener. And he reemphasizes in *From the Diary of a Snail* his belief in the essential identity of all violent behavior.

During the public outcry following the appearance of an article by Heinrich Böll in *Der Spiegel* magazine that appeared to be a defense of the Baader-Meinhof gang, Grass devoted one of his columns in the *Süddeutsche Zeitung* to the question. He is especially sensitive, Grass writes, to violent trends on the left "because I am hit at close range by that which is recognizable under its leftist foretokens as a method of the right, still verbal or already violent" (BS 243). He is deferential to Böll as a friend and colleague, but he does not hesitate to lecture him on his errors, reiterating in the process many of the political arguments of *Local Anaesthetic* and *From the Diary of a Snail.*

CHAPTER SIX

The Flounder
(Der Butt)

IN THE MIDDLE OF HIS SNAIL DIARY, THE CAMPAIGN-weary Grass inserts four wistful lines, hinting that someday, "before I grow old and possibly wise," he would like to rest from his political travails for a while and write a book about something he really enjoys: "I want to write a narrating cookbook: about 99 dishes, about guests, and humans as animals that can cook" (AT 212).

He kept up his busy schedule even after 1972, with numerous regional campaigns, political speeches, and essays. He made trips to the Soviet Union, Greece, France, Italy, Israel, the United States, Canada, Poland, India, and eventually also to the Far East and to Africa. His editorial efforts included the founding with Heinrich Böll and Carola Stern of the journal *L'76 Demokratie und Sozialismus: Politische und Literarische Beiträge* (L'76 Democracy and Socialism: Political and Literary Contributions), as well as a later publishing firm called L'80 (hereafter the journal was also called *L'80*). He supervised the publication of collected editions of his poems, his plays, and another volume of his speeches and essays entitled *Der Bürger und seine Stimme* (The Citizen and His Voice). He received an honorary doctorate from Harvard. And he worked to develop a model agreement with the publishing firm of Luchterhand to provide authors with greatly increased rights of participation in important publication decisions. But despite the crush of everyday political affairs Grass did in fact begin to write his cookbook.

It was well under way when in 1974 events conspired to make Grass shift the balance of his life back even more in the direction of the arts. Chancellor Willy Brandt resigned following the revelation that his assistant Günther Guillaume was an East German spy. Grass had anticipated exactly this kind of discouragement in the Dürer speech on standing still in progress. Saddened but more determined than ever, he proclaimed the snail had left us behind and we must work even harder to catch up to her.

The "cookbook" appeared in 1977 as *The Flounder*. At almost the same length, 700 pages, it is a book with, if anything, an even more complex narrative fabric and an even wider epic scope than *The Tin Drum* and *Dog Years*, since it harks back to neolithic times, over two millennia B.C.

Of course it is set in Danzig, or in the region on the Vistula called Pomerania (named after its inhabitants the Pomorshians), that will become Giotheschants, Gidanie, Gdancyk, Danczik, Dantzig, Danzig, and then Gdansk. Oskar puts in an appearance, of course, just as there is a suspiciously large number of eyeglasses (shades of Brauxel) belonging to the most visionary characters. Many previous historical allusions, including the story of the young revolutionary Bartholdy from *Local Anaesthetic,* are finally fully expounded.

126

The narrator is a man, whose identification with Grass himself appears to fall only a little short of that in *From the Diary of a Snail*. Yet even there, it should be recalled, Grass freely fictionalized his own life, and creations such as Hermann Ott also bear an autobiographical stamp. It is significant that the narrator is *not* totally or simply identical to Grass: as a kind of archetypal male per se, he is present in over twenty transmogrifications throughout the ages. He is often present as two, three, or even six men living at the same time, always with a friend whose name contains the syllable Lud or Lad (Ludek, Ludger, Ladewig, Ludewik, Ludwig, Ludström), a memorial to Grass's deceased friend the sculptor Ludwig Gabriel Schrieber. In his latest avatar he is a Social Democratic writer living—like Grass—in Wewelsfleth near Itzehoe, married to a shrewlike and glassbreaking woman named Ilsebill.

The Flounder begins with a meal, prepared by the man and the woman, and, since it is fundamentally a study in yin and yang, with a double impregnation. The male narrator physically penetrates his wife Ilsebill, who metaphysically penetrates him: "As if in compensation her feeling penetrated, thrusting, my feeling: doubled, we were diligent" (DB 10).

Both pregnancies, the physical and the metaphysical, as well as world history from the Stone Age to the present, gestate and grow in the book's nine "months" or sections. At the end of the ninth month history begets our present world. Ilsebill bears a physical child (based on Grass's own daughter Helena, who was born in 1974 and to whom *The Flounder* is dedicated). The narrator, like Zeus, brings forth his metaphysical "headbirth" (a later offshoot from *The Flounder* also has this word in its title). This is equivalent to the bringing forth of the novel itself, or to the bringing forth of its central insight, an extrapolative prediction from history about the future of life on our planet.

One strand of the narrative deals with previous embodiments of the narrator, his male friends, and his women, the cooks, from Neolithic times to the present, told by the narrator to his present wife, Ilsebill. Another strand involves the flounder (or, more correctly, the tur*bot*, a word whose final syllable, like that of hali*but*—"holy butt"—is cognate to *Butt*): he is the fish of the fairy tale "The Fisherman and his Wife." The tale was told by an old woman to the romantic painter Phillip Otto Runge and later published by the Brothers Grimm. It is, of course, the source of the name Ilsebill. Another zoomorphic reification of the *Zeitgeist*, or in this case the *Weltgeist* (world spirit), like Grass's snail or dog, this flounder advises the male narrator and his subsequent incarnations down through the centuries until, in our day, he changes sides and advises the women.

His dual role as adviser, like the double impregnation, has its analogue in dual versions of the fairy tale. In *The Flounder* we learn there were originally two equally valid versions of the story: the conventional one, in which the insatiably ambitious and acquisitive person is a woman, Ilsebill, and a lost version, in which it is a man. The latter version is destroyed by Runge and the Grimms out of fear it might undermine the prevailing pattern of male dominance.

At first, the flounder is not simply consulted by the

women when he allows himself to be caught by them; he is placed on trial for his male chauvinist crimes against humanity. Another important strand of narration, then, relates the empaneling of a *femin*ist tribun*al* or *feminal* and the interrogation of the fish. Members of this modern feminal correspond to historical female cooks in much the same way the narrative "I" corresponds to their previous male companions. In them, all phases of history and all shadings of ideology are simultaneously present and interactive.

Another major strand of narrative is that consisting of forty-six poems, dispersed between chapters throughout the months of the book, except in the eighth month. This is reserved in its entirety for a shocking tale of rape and murder unrelieved by poetry. The poems recapitulate, on a more cryptic, hermetic level, all the other strands of narrative.

The first cook is Aua (Awe in the English edition), who has, the narrator swears, three breasts. Actually, he recalls, all women in the clan in that age, including Ilsebill, were named Aua and had three breasts. All the men in the clan were called Edek, including the narrator, who was a fisherman and a sculptor specializing in fired-clay images of the three-breasted mother goddess Aua. It would be difficult to miss—yet many have—the tone of ironic playfulness with which Grass limns this whimsical matriarchal world. He pokes fun at what serious literary critics have diagnosed in him—partly because of Oskar's infantilism—as a chronic, chthonic mother complex. On the Old Prussian east side of the river he hastens to assure an angry Ilsebill, balancing the

equation (and evoking Eddi Amsel in the process)
there was a man named Potrimpos. He became a
Prussian god along with Pikollos and Perkunos, and
is said to have had three testicles.

That modern mortals have only two breasts or
testicles is a capricious symbol in *The Flounder* for
the fact that something, some dialectic dimension,
some mythical echo of the lost trinity, is missing:
"It's true the third one is often lacking today. I mean
something is lacking. Well, the third thing" (DB 11).
Two pages further on, the narrator continues,
"Perhaps we have just forgotten that there is something else. A third something. Also in other ways,
also politically, as a possibility" (DB 13).

Whatever this third something represents, modern
feminists, like Amazons, have even less of it, the
narrator maintains: "With her three thingamabobs
Aua overdid it just as much as the Amazons under-
did it with their one single breast. For which reason
the feminists today always go to the other extreme"
(DB 12).

In this primitive Pomorshian paradise on the Vistula the Auas amply nurse, nourish, and nurture the
clan, including the adult males. On the simplest
level, their plethora of breasts, which "rose as hills
in the landscape" (DB 11), is a symbol for their identity with Gaea, the Earth Mother. Women rule there
because the primeval Aua has stolen fire from the
sky wolf and carried the coals back to earth in her
vagina. (This is an adaptation of South American Indian myths cited in *The Raw and the Cooked* by
Claude Lévi-Strauss.[1]) The name Aua itself sounds
like and memorializes her cries of pain. But she

allows the fire to be used only for warmth, for cooking, or, in the case of Edek, the artist-narrator, for the firing of clay figures.

It is the talking fish, the Promethean principle, caught by Edek the narrator for the first time, who suggests the masculine idea that the sacred cooking fires can be used also for smelting metals out of certain stones. "Notice, my son! Metal can be hammered into spear points and axes" (DB 36).

These Stone Age hunters have stone weapons, of course, but whenever Edeks encounter Ludeks, the men of another clan, they hastily confer with Aua, as the Ludeks confer with their Eua or Eia, and hostilities cease as dinner invitations are exchanged: "War was not declared, but everyone was invited to the table" (DB 80). When the women discover the men have fashioned bronze weapons, they are angry and throw the weapons into the river after a ritual dance around an image of the three-breasted goddess.

Edek, sorrowing at the loss of the metal weapons, again calls upon the fish, who tells him Aua has secretly kept a bronze kitchen knife and he should kill her with it. Edek declines, for though it is the scientific and technical knowledge gained through his secret contacts with the fish which gradually erodes the paradise, an Edek does not commit the first murder: it is a woman, Mestwina, the tenth-century incarnation of Aua, who kills the Christian bishop Adalbert of Prague.

This cook's weapon is a cast-iron cooking spoon. It is a metallic perversion of the nourishing female principle, an echo of the weapon wielded by Walter Matern's violent grandmother. From now forward, the metallic, life-taking male principle will infringe upon the organic, life-giving female principle, and the two will be at odds, even in women: black cooks will alternate with white cooks, often within the same person.

Grass's cooks will alternately introduce the potato to Prussia under Friedrich II, thus staving off hunger (Amanda Woyke), and feed poisonous mushrooms to French occupation troops under Napoleon (Sophie Rotzoll). They will smother a lover in bed during the Reformation (Margarete—"Fat Gret"—Rusch), and feed Jews and other prisoners in the death camp at Stutthof during the Third Reich (Lena Stubbe).

These cooks, each in her setting, with her male companion or companions, are all briefly introduced in the first pages of the novel. They are episodically reintroduced at certain stages throughout the book, and then, in the month specifically dedicated to each one and to her time, dealt with more completely. In order to fit eleven cooks into nine months, however, Grass places the first three, all pagans of the Vistula estuary, living before the conversion of the Pomorshians to Christianity and the founding of the city of Danzig, into the first month.

The first, and only totally complete cook, the only one with three breasts, is, as we have seen, Aua. Her counterpart on the feminal is Frau Dr. Ursula Schönherr, the presiding judge, even the meaning of whose last name, "beautiful lord," has matriarchal overtones harking back to Aua. She casts the sole dissenting vote against a resolution condemning as impractical and unthinkable the important symbolical concept of three breasts.

The second cook is the two-breasted Iron Age priestess Wigga. How Wigga and the other women of her time came to be lacking the third breast is unclear, but the narrator offers several possibilities. One is that since her father was a Goth named Ludolf, not a Pomorshian, Wigga is herself part heir to his Germanic, patriarchal nature, and therefore one breast short of perfection.

In any event, the loss of the previously absolute, three-breasted matriarchy has its equivalents in other cultures and mythologies. (Hera is forced to marry Zeus and to grant dominion over the sea to Poseidon, here the classical equivalent of the new Pomorshian flounder-god Ryb.) And it has a dark, counterrevolutionary side: female perversions of the primordial matriarchy spring up in the form of Amazons, Bacchantes, Erinyes, Maenads, Sirens, and Medusas—in Grass's mythology the classical equivalents of modern female terrorists.

Under the part-Germanic Wigga, who herself has the wrinkled aspect of a turnip, this society of hunters and gatherers develops into one of agriculturalists, using masculine, metallic tools to plow and plant. They raise primarily edible roots such as primitive varieties of red beet and radish, all descended from a phallic *Urwurzel* (primordial root), a vegetative symbol of the inexorable rise of the phallusocracy. The East Germanic Goths, who have conquered the area in that historic migration known as the *Völkerwanderung,* scornfully call the Pomorshians root eaters, who in return make prophetic references to the warlike Goths as iron eaters.

Yet bored and frustrated under their peacefully

polyandrous and herbivorous matriarchy, some Pomorshian men are infected by the excitement of the bellicose and nomadic life of these monogamous, patriarchal, and carnivorous Goths. They join them on their military adventures—called profascist by the feminal, a suggestion that this is also a symbol of wars to come—only to limp back later (among other insults Edek has been sodomized by an old Goth in a horned helmet) to their matriarchal roots. Because their military foray was so singularly unsuccessful, Helga Paasch, Wigga's modern counterpart on the feminal—she has radish-colored hair, we learn— votes this time for leniency for the flounder, who had helped arrange it.

After the departure for the south of the Goths, who were faced with the bleak prospect of spending a hard winter sharing the Pomorshians' vegetarian diet, no significant changes occur among the people of the Vistula estuary until the tenth century, with the arrival from Bohemia of the Christian missionary bishop Adalbert of Prague. The Pomorshian priestess Mestwina, who is engaged by the Bohemian entourage as a cook, falls in love with this ascetic sourpuss, another of the narrator's incarnations. (In his simultaneous incarnation as a shepherd, in anticipation of the tribe's imminent conversion, the narrator begins to carve figures of the Virgin, albeit with three breasts beneath her folds.)

Adalbert remains cool toward Mestwina until one day her amber necklace accidentally breaks and is dissolved in the fish soup she is cooking for his fast. The aphrodisiacal power of the pagan amber, ostensibly imparted to it by the new male flounder-god

Ryb, turns his piety into priapism, and he demonstrates an insatiable appetite both for Mestwina's ample flesh and for her soup of amber and fish.

Yet he remains opposed to the pagan rites of the clan, such as that in which fish heads are carried atop long poles back to the sea in a solemn procession, with the head of Ryb going on before. When Adalbert commands his men to re-decapitate these satanic heads, Mestwina becomes angry, chews muscarine-laden mushrooms, quaffs a quantity of fermented mare's milk and, thus emboldened, kills Adalbert with his own cast-iron cooking spoon, which she had been using as a milk ladle.

Betrayed by the narrator in his incarnation as the shepherd-sculptor, Mestwina is beheaded. Her execution by Adalbert's successor Ludewig and the subsequent forced baptism of the Pomorshians mark the official end of the matriarchal society descended from Aua. But much of its fundamental feminine nature remains intact in the person of the cooks, handed down clandestinely from mother to daughter and granddaughter, or subsumed into the cult of the Virgin, kept alive in no small part by the narrator's three-breasted images with their amber eyes.

Mestwina's contemporary counterpart on the feminal is Ruth Simoneit, who wears an amber necklace and, because she drinks, has the same glassy-eyed look as Mestwina when she had imbibed too much fermented mare's milk. The account of Mestwina's homicidal deed inspires the more radical elements of the tribunal to unite into a revolutionary faction advocating a violent end to the phallusocracy.

After the death of Mestwina and the canonization

of St. Adalbert, the Polish duke Boleslav, who had enlisted Adalbert's help in converting the pagans, made the Vistula estuary into a province called Pomerania, after the Pomorshians, whom Boleslav now condescendingly calls Kashubians. In the thirteenth century, then, amid the deadly masculine struggles between various Kashubian dukes named Mestwin and Swantopolk, the Teutonic Knights, the Poles, and the Dukes of Brandenburg—all of which are directly echoed in later battles, from the Thirty Years' War, through Napoleon and Hitler, to the bloody Polish food strikes of 1970—the city of Danzig is founded. Built around the ancient wicker bastion of the Pomorshians, it is the home of the fourth cook, Dorothea of Montau, the subject of Grass's second month, and her husband, the narrator Albrecht Slichting.

As the first of Grass's cooks to live entirely under a patriarchy, Dorothea is the first total victim of male dominance. But she is also—hence her inclusion—the first woman to revolt against the patriarchal coercion of medieval marriage. Her husband, a maker of phallic (metallic) swords, gets her pregnant eight times in a row—once with twins—and strikes her when she is not as submissive as he thinks a woman should be. To be free she really only has two choices, we read, religious mania or witchcraft, and she chooses the former.

Danzig needs a home-grown saint in order to be able to compete militarily and economically with the Swedes and the Poles, who have their own saints Birgitta and Hedwig. So it is decided by the local male political leaders that this religious seer—she accurately foretells the downfall of the Teutonic Knights, for example—who cares for lepers and feeds the poor, should prematurely die and then be canonized.

Dorothea's modern counterpart on the feminal is the prosecutor, Dr. Sieglinda "Siggi" Huntscha, one of the women who catch the flounder for the second time. She is linked to Dorothea among other things by the wheat-colored blondness of her hair, in turn linking both of them to ancient cereal goddesses like Demeter.

The final speech to the feminal on the case by the wise Aua figure, Dr. Schönherr, is an important summary of the status of the old female, nourishing principle under the new patriarchy: "Since Dorothea men have tried either to canonize women's desire for freedom or to dismiss it as typical female craziness" (DB 183).

Grass begins the third month, dedicated to the fifth cook, the abbess Margarete "Fat Gret" Rusch, with an account of his trip to India. Here he imagines himself as Gret's contemporary Vasco da Gama, the European discoverer of the subcontinent, whose successors henceforth supply spices to the kitchens of Europe. He encounters the four-armed goddess Kali, violent, death-dealing feminine perversion of three-breasted Aua. In Kali's name Indian women are more and more fruitful, but this results in starvation rather than satiation. Her latest horrible avatar might well be the hardened political realist, the (masculine) female prime minister Indira

Ghandi. Under Kali's awful aegis a perversion of the Stone Age has returned, with primitive people hunkering before cooking fires on the pavements of Calcutta.

The abbess Fat Gret, this plump, goose-plucking polyandrist, is the corpulent counterpole to the emaciated Indians. Her father, another of the narrator's metalworking male incarnations, is a blacksmith who has been sentenced to death for his political and theological agitation against the Catholic patrician class. But Gret is not a complete Aua, a life-giver and life-sustainer. As the daughter of a blacksmith, she can play at lethal men's games as well. She promises her father she will avenge herself on his two main enemies. She suffocates the wealthy patrician mayor Ferber in her bed and stuffs the abbot Jescke to death with rich dishes, thus using the life-giving female attributes, sexuality and gastronomy, to take life.

This, however, according to the flounder, was an unfortunate failing in an otherwise almost exemplary matriarchal goddess. He recommends a system of secular feminist cloisters modeled on hers to liberate women from patriarchal *Bettzwang* (bed coercion) and provide a strong economic base of operations. His recommendations have that utopian glow so often warned of by Grass, and they seem only to imitate what men had already created in their fraternal organizations. Yet when one subtracts from the flounder's words a certain residual male cynicism— later the penitent flounder seems to drop all such pretenses—they do serve as a reminder of the exis-

tence of Grass's distant, dialectic goal based on a
harmony of life-giving and life-sustaining principles.

Gret's present-day counterpart is the organist Ulla
Witzlaff. She is also a descendant of the old woman
who told Phillip Otto Runge the two versions of the
fairy tale.

After the pagan cooks, the High Gothic ascetic
cook, and the lusty Reformation cook, there follows
in the fourth month the sixth, baroque cook, the
angelic Agnes Kurbiella. She is likewise a personification of her age, the (Thirty Years') war-ravaged,
yet highly spiritually refined seventeenth century.
Agnes's two male consorts are likewise more refined,
no longer artisans like their predecessors, but histor-
ically significant artists: the painter Anton Möller
and the poet Martin Opitz.

Themselves nearly ruined in both body and spirit
by the stresses of the age, these two artists discover,
sitting vacantly before the church, a young goose-girl
who has been raped and whose family has been murdered by Swedish marauders. To these artists she becomes the gentle barefoot cook, the mistress, and the
polyandric muse. She is more spiritually refined than
both of them together, an eternal feminine wellspring of all the arts: Rubens and Hölderlin, it is
said, could not have exhausted her supply of aesthetic inspiration or of unconditional love.

The flounder testifies he had originally introduced
the principle of love into the paradisiacal matriarchy
in order to destroy it by creating jealousy, then
monandry, male dominance, and female submissive-
ness. Now the flounder calls on the feminal to emu-

late Agnes, saying it will be the power of woman's love which will change the world one day.

His speech is interrupted by angry feminists, who unplug his microphone. But some of the women are deeply touched, and from this day forth a supportive minority, the "flounder party," as it is called, exists in the feminal. It includes, for a time at least, Agnes's modern-day alter ego the defense counsel Bettina von Carnow. She will bring up the subject of love again and judge future cooks on the basis of this great quality as well.

As befitting her divine charity and angelic inner beauty, the muse Agnes is burned as a witch by the religious and political powers of the day. After the death of Möller and Opitz, Grass has her follow another famous baroque poet, the visionary Quirinus Kuhlmann, to his death at the stake in Moscow. In fact, all the true goddesses might have been, and yet might be, flayed alive and then burned as witches, the narrator says, for the cruel impulse is yet found in man. In their great self-sacrificing love, however, even before the concept of love is introduced, the goddesses gladly give their bodies to be burned, and even to be eaten in communion: as the original Aua, here called Überaua (Superaua), caused her body to be cooked and eaten by the clan during an especially harsh famine.

Another attribute shared by Agnes with her sister goddesses is that she is also a clairvoyant, a seer. In the fourth month we learn one way such seers foresee the future, one way they gain their higher insights into the nature of all things, is by examining

140

excrement. This is an extension of the ancient practice of examining entrails, especially those of birds, by the (masculine) *haruspex*, (feminine) *haruspica*, literally: intestine seer. It seems a logical thing for the cooks to do, considering they are responsible for the total well-being of their men and children, which includes proper digestion of the food they prepare.

With his Grassian flair for turning ordinary nausea into a higher moral principle, in these passages the narrator recommends to Ilsebill a return to a more harmonious, natural, even coprophagous relationship to the product of digestion, such as that enjoyed by small children. (She has broken off and swallowed a tooth with a gold crown, but is ashamed to look through her excrement to find it.) Then, as an *haruspica* herself, he says, she might find hidden treasures of truth, hidden, holistic knowledge about all aspects of her life and her times. She may even learn about something political—based on the inspection of babies' diapers—such as the need to boycott the Nestlé company for promoting a profitable but pernicious preference for infant formula over mother's milk in Third World nations.

Grass's fifth month is dedicated to his seventh cook, Amanda Woyke, who lives during the eighteenth century, the age of that enlightened despot Friedrich II of Prussia. Her common-law husband is August Romeike, one of Friedrich's veterans and an inspector for the Royal State Farms. In Grass's history it is she, not Friedrich the Great—or Old Fritz, as he is known—who is credited with introducing the potato to Prussia. And through her correspondence

141

with Benjamin Thompson, Count Rumford, the Europeanized Anglo-American officer and inventor, she also spreads it to other parts of Germany such as Bavaria.

The potato is her panacea, her answer to famine, which has taken her three small daughters, Stine, Trude, and Lovise, as well as to its concomitant evils, military campaigns and pestilence. Amanda, like the other cooks, is a great storyteller, an inexhaustible wellspring of narrative wisdom. Fittingly, her protracted narratives are spun out like the potato peelings she continuously creates. (One is reminded that Grass originally intended *Dog Years* to be called *Potato Peelings*.) The other cooks' narrative styles also grow out of their respective activities: Mestwina stamps acorns in a mortar and produces short chopped sentences, Fat Gret light, feathery ones as she plucks geese.

Each in her own style, the cooks here retell all the old stories, adding some additional information in the process: After the theft of his fire, the sky wolf comes to earth in the form of a flounder, teaches men to make iron spears, kill the cooks, and bring war to the earth. That is why Amanda always concludes her stories about marauding soldiers of whatever nationality with the words: "They was like wolves" (DB 373).

This visionary matriarch foresees the establishment of a worldwide system of communal kitchens, which efficiently and adequately feed everyone. When Friedrich pays an unexpected visit to the farm, she warms, dries, and mothers the broken old warrior, and feeds him her famous never-ending potato soup. She lobbies him to wage in the future nothing but *Kartoffelschlachten* (potato battles) against hunger, to give parcels of land back to the peasants for the raising of potatoes, and to establish communal kitchens throughout the land.

Her vision is not attained. "After Amanda's death darkness fell upon Europe," the flounder says (DB 411). But in the form of a fairy tale "Why Potato Soup Tastes Divine" he tells the feminal what happened when Amanda died and went to heaven. There she begins to search for God, but instead she finds her little girls, Stine, Trude, and Lovise, in the form of mealworms in a great celestial flour bin, which is otherwise empty. They had starved because Old Fritz had been waging his Seven Years' War.

She pushes the bin along until she comes to Old Fritz, playing war with his little tin soldiers, attempting with peppercorns as cannonballs to win the lost battle of Kolin. Amanda hitches the king to the bin, puts the tin soldiers inside, and marches forward until she finds Count Rumford, who has invented a machine to process the primordial energy of hellfire into handy heat tablets. She takes him and his invention along. They encounter the narrator, August Romeike, the ne'er-do-well veteran and father of her children, who has managed to take with him into heaven one bag of seed potatoes and a few herbs.

When they arrive at the sea, Amanda calls out for God, but the flounder appears instead, and in answer to her request turns the celestial halls into rolling Kashubian fields of sandy loam, plowed and ready for planting. The tin soldiers leap out of the bin and begin to farm. Rumford builds a great kitchen. The little mealworms grow up into beautiful girls. They all live happily ever after, without any need for the king to rule—his useless and dangerous cannonballs are rolled into hell, whereupon it provides even more heat tablets—the count to invent or the inspector to inspect.

This remarkable allegory with its lyrical counterpart in the fifth month, the touching poem "Plaint and Prayer of the Farm Cook Amanda Woyke" encapsulates the entire novel. It has a powerful effect on the women of the feminal, more and more of whom are moved to join the flounder party. Amanda's modern-day correspondent, Therese Osslieb, converts her posh Czech-Viennese-style restaurant into a plain farm kitchen called Ilsebill's Shack. There potato soup and other basic dishes are served along with ample portions of motherly affection and education about world hunger.

The eighth cook, the subject of the sixth month, is Amanda's granddaughter, the angelic Sophie Rotzoll. As befitting her romantic age, the age of Napoleon, her chapter is replete with mysterious dark forests, full moons, fairy tales, and mind-expanding mushrooms. Sophie is an expert on mushrooms, having learned about them at her grandmother Amanda's knee.

Sophie's friend Friedrich "Fritz" Bartholdy, whom we encountered briefly before in *Local Anaesthetic*, is now serving a life sentence for his role in an aborted uprising inspired by the French Revolution. She has made Fritz's years in his cold, damp cell more bearable by sending him cakes into which was baked powdered fly agaric, that mushroom containing a nonlethal dose of the extremely poisonous psychedelic agent muscarine.

When Napoleon and his troops enter Danzig, Sophie falls on her knees before his Imperial Majesty and entreats him to release Bartholdy. She is referred to a cynical adjutant, General Rapp. When he eventually becomes the governor of the city, he hires the beautiful Sophie as his cook, cruelly offering her the release of her friend—to whom she has pledged her chastity and eternal loyalty—in exchange for sexual favors.

Sophie finally sees no other choice but to kill Rapp, a private act symbolizing the overthrow, in all Europe, of the oppressive Napoleonic yoke. She prepares a calf's head stuffed with mushrooms. Rapp has been warned by the flounder not to eat this muscarine-laden delicacy, so he is spared; but his dinner guests, all allied officers and other potentates, partake, go berserk, and cut each other to ribbons.

A woman, Queen Luise of Prussia, finally grants Sophie's request, and Fritz is released, after thirty-eight years. He is a broken, quiet old man—a regular consumer of fly agaric—who together with Sophie operates a mushroom stand at the marketplace.

Naturally the feminal discusses at length the use of poisonous mushrooms as a feminine tool of political assassination. The druggist Griselde Dubertin, Sophie's counterpart and one of the several more radical women who favor the proposition, gives lectures on toxicology: "Poison's the only remedy!" she says (DB 494). Sieglinde Huntscha agrees, though she complains that Sophie had allowed Rapp to escape unharmed. Ruth Simoneit favors less subtle methods: "I'm in favor of beating them to death. Out in the open! Slam-bam!" (DB 494).

Grass's ninth cook, of the seventh month, is Lena Stobbe or Stubbe, née Pipka, another distant relative of Amanda Woyke. Her life corresponds exactly to the history of the workers' movement, from her birth just after the revolutions of 1848 to her death in the concentration camp at Stutthof in 1942. Each of her completely interchangeable drunken, brutal, anchor-maker husbands, Friedrich Otto Stobbe and Otto Friedrich Stubbe, dies at the very beginning of a major European exercise in virility, the Franco-Prussian War of 1870–71 and the First World War of 1914–18.

To each of them, and to all the other members of society, this seer was an exemplar of and a living monument to the loyal, loving, nourishing, long-suffering, female, socialist principle. When her man tries to hang himself, for example, she cuts him down and feeds him and all the other men henceforth a magical homeopathic soup—and other dishes—in which she cooks the spike and the rope from the hanging, hence comforting the men and reducing their suicidal impulses.

With her magical eyeglasses—with which she also examines excrement—this seer Lena ends her life at Stutthof, having spent most of her ninety-three years nourishing her fellow human beings. Near the end she cooks for the poor Jews waiting in vain for their visas to the United States and for the Nazi "winter help" feeding program, ignoring political differences to be able to feed the hungry. Finally the "crazy old

146

woman" cooks for forced laborers from the Ukraine, with whom she shares the arm band reading *OST* (EAST).

When she is taken to Stutthof she feeds the prisoners there for almost a year before being brutally murdered by criminal elements trying to steal her supplies. Her broken glasses are found next to her battered corpse, upon which rats, in a starkly consistent extension of her role as Aua, the provider of nourishment, have been feeding.

Lena's long life spans the borderline between the historical past and the present. Hence there is only a subtle link between her and her present counterpart on the feminal, Erika Nöttke. The last two present cooks, Sibylle Miehlau and Maria Kuczorra, also have only a faint link to members of the feminal, Beate Hagedorn and Elisabeth Güllen, respectively. Grass nevertheless establishes a link, apparently in order to underscore, as he always had in previous works, the exact parallel between the fictional past and the real present.

The narrator ends the seventh month—which brings the book up to the present era—with a summary of the violent deaths of all but two of the historical cooks. He proposes to devote the next month to an account of the more recent death of Lena's granddaughter Sibylle Miehlau. But the flounder counsels him to end the book here, at the end of the past, not wishing to take the responsibility for further atrocities in the present or future. At this the narrator cries out: "No, Flounder! No! The book goes on and so does history" (DB 572).

As we have repeatedly seen in these historical months, though the male principle has gained power and control, it can never totally eradicate the female, which lives on tenaciously in the previously untold history of cooking. And the bankruptcy of the male principle is near at hand. As predicted in the destroyed version of the fairy tale, after man has built bridges over the widest rivers, phallic torpedoes, rockets, and towers that reach to the clouds, has learned to fly, and wants to journey to the distant stars, all his efforts will collapse: "All the majesty, towers, bridges, and flying machines collapse, the dikes break, drought follows, sandstorms ravage, the mountains spew fire, old mother earth shakes off, by quaking, the dominion of man" (DB 443).

Even the flounder, now almost transparent, glasslike, or astral, penitent, and in the process of being reborn as the feminine *Weltgeist*, is disgusted and deserts his sons: "Your era is ending on a sour note. In short: Man is finished. . . . Whether in capitalism or in Communism: everywhere madness is doing the reasoning" (DB 572).

But who, if anyone, will take over history from the men? Certainly not those women who cut off their symbolical breasts like Amazons, go berserk like the Erinyes, Maenads, or Medusas, who merely imitate men, *The Flounder* maintains. If they do, the attainment of equality between the sexes would only raise the sum of all male striving to the second power, we read. This scenario is grotesquely and graphically anticipated in the eighth month, subtitled "Father's Day."

Here the (tenth) cook is Sibylle Miehlau, the

granddaughter of Lena Stubbe, the heroic old Social Democrat who died at Stutthof. Sibylle is the narrator's former fiancée and the mother of his child. But she has given the child to its grandmother to raise, has become a lesbian, and has masculinized her name to Billy. (Continued sexual brutality at the hands of men—as a fourteen-year old she was raped by Russian soldiers—is the reason for her decision.)

Today, Ascension Day, she is on her way to the lake for a traditional Father's Day picnic—for men only!—with three friends, Fränki, Siggi, and Mäxchen, the very women who later catch the flounder, all of them dressed in men's clothing. Singing a symbolical song of hunger—unlike the cooks who always celebrate satiation—they pretend to be men who have lived in all ages of the past. They pretend to have raped and impregnated the past cooks, thus recapitulating in one more way all the previous episodes.

During the bizarre course of events Mäxchen and eventually Siggi and Fränki rape Billy with a dildo. This is a grotesque and vainly impotent effort to sire a new, mythical *Übersohn* (super son), a savior figure named Emmanuel (the "God with us" of Isaiah 7:14 and Matthew 1:23). The event is linked to Ascension Day by being portrayed as a bit of a crucifixion, a killing of a savior rather than the siring of one. Such violent "masculine" treatment awakens Sibylle to her woman- and motherhood. The seer dons her symbolic eyeglasses, sees the truth, and leaves her "friends" crying "I am a woman, a woman, a woman!" (DB 623).

A motorcycle gang in black leather has observed

this "really filthy abomination" from their chrome-plated (metallic) cycles (DB 617). Aroused, these sharks, these seven "black angels," gang-rape her, which is a communion to them, we read. Then they run their heavy machines repeatedly over her body, reducing it to pulp, with her broken glasses, like those of her grandmother, lying nearby.

This episode, possibly the starkest and most shocking thing Grass has ever written, closely parallels that in *Dog Years* where Eddi and Jenny are attacked by Walter and Tulla, the male and female personifications of evil. Eleven of the same crows here also serve as witnesses and link the shameful events. It demonstrates not only the bankruptcy of the male principle but that of the "one-breasted" militant Amazonian female principle as well, and the extent to which it has become corrupted by the male.

But it also demonstrates that in extremis, when the absurdity of male striving after power is most clearly revealed, when it is even raised by females to the second power, the fundamental "three-breasted" female impulse may emerge again. It could take control of history from henceforth, as predicted by the flounder: "History demands a feminine imprint. The turning point of time!" (DB 662). It could also give birth to a truly new breed of human, "who, untainted by privilege and power, would be brand-new" (DB 14), thus providing the dialectic third possibility: a harmonious synthesis of the sexes.

It will not be brought about by conventional female leaders—Madame Pompadour, Golda Meir, and Indira Ghandi are mentioned—who merely place politics in the procrustean bed of male historical consciousness. It will be opposed by radical feminists, such as that life-taking minority on the feminal who cast a vote for the death penalty for the flounder and then cast stones at the others who return the flounder to the sea. (After his full, final confession to the crimes of history the life-giving majority decide to celebrate the passing of the old god by holding a symbolical communal meal of eleven common flounders and then return their future counselor henceforth to his element.) For these female terrorists—one is reminded here of Ulrike Meinhof—history has gone back full circle to the Stone Age, with the masculinized women this time using stone weapons.

For the other women, for the true cooks like the eleventh, Maria Kuczorra, the subject of the ninth month, history moves ahead, not backward. It does not move in utopian leaps—*From the Diary of a Snail* settled that issue—but slowly, surely, with the help of a transfigured feminine flounder, or snail. (Like-minded men are by no means excluded on the basis of their sex: Maria's common-law husband Jan Ludkowski is shot down by troops in front of the Lenin shipyards in Gdansk during the strikes in 1970 over food (!) prices.)

On the last pages of the novel the narrator visits Maria in Gdansk. He follows her along the beach. She, not he, initiates their sexual intercourse. They eat the food she has cooked. Then she runs out into the sea and calls out a Kashubian word, loudly, three times, whereupon a flounder—not the old flounder, we are told, but a new one, her flounder—leaps into her arms and speaks with her for a considerable time. The male narrator sits on the beach, "Fallen out of history" as he describes himself (DB 693).

When Maria returns, it is not Maria, though it appears to be—nor any of the other cooks, whom she resembles—but Ilsebill, a synthesis of all the cooks: "Ilsebill came. She overlooked me, overstepped me. Already she had passed me by. I ran after her" (DB 694).

This ending, like that of *The Tin Drum*, points ahead to the future. There, Oskar feared he would always have the Black Cook, the personification of the evil principle, coming toward him, confronting him. Here, the male narrator runs after the (white) cook, the personification of the new, nourishing female principle. She has broken out of the vicious circle of war and starvation and has begun to make the future history of the world a potential history, at least, of peace and plenty.

Needless to say, reception of *The Flounder* was anything but unanimous or blasé. Though it is much more critical of men than of women—that is the main point of the novel, after all—some feminists hated it.[2] And to the extent they missed his ironic self-abnegation and the subtle mythical differences between Günter Grass and the narrators, to the extent the close autobiographical ties led them exactly to equate the two, they hated Günter Grass as well, and said so.

Those readers who had been shocked by Grass's use of obscenity and vulgarity before were, of course, even more disgusted by the unabashed and graphic inclusion in a book about gastronomy of such sub-

jects as coprophagia and cunnilingus. Many failed to
see the logic of Grass's mythical way of thinking.
They failed to appreciate his tradition of linking
shocking "immoral" personal behavior (such as Fat
Gret's eucharist) to *truly* immoral historical events
(such as those lethal disputes about transubstantia-
tion and real presence that led to religious wars). Yet
the novel was so widely acclaimed and sold so many
copies that Grass, suffering from an embarrassment
of riches, was in 1978 able to endow, after only one
year, a literary award in the name of his admired
"teacher" Alfred Döblin, administered by the Berlin
Academy of Art.

It appears Grass's concern for the historical and
mythological battle of the sexes may have been in
part suggested by his private life. During the writing
of *The Flounder* his marriage had been crumbling,
and in 1978 it ended in divorce. The next year he
married the Berlin organist Ute Ehrhardt Grunert,
the model for the character in the novel named Ulla
Witzlaff.

With her he made a trip through Asia, an account
of which would provide the autobiographical skeleton
for a shorter diary on the model of *From the Diary of
a Snail* entitled *Kopfgeburten oder Die Deutschen
sterben aus* (*Headbirths or The Germans Are Dying
Out*, 1980). In the meantime he had worked on a film
version of *The Tin Drum* with director Volker
Schlöndorff, who with his actress-director wife Mar-
garethe von Trotta also accompanied Grass to the
Orient. When the film appeared in 1979 it won the
Golden Palm at Cannes. Grass had himself won
several more literary prizes, including two important

Italian awards, the International Mondello Prize in 1977 and the Viareggio Prize in 1978.

NOTES

1. See Scott H. Abbott, "The Raw and the Cooked: Claude Lévi-Strauss and Günter Grass" *The Fisherman and His Wife: Günter Grass's "The Flounder" in Critical Perspective*, ed. Siegfried Mews (New York: AMS Press, 1983), 107–20.

2. See, e.g., Ruth K. Angress, *"Der Butt*—A Feminist Perspective," *Adventures of a Flounder: Critical Essays on Günter Grass' "Der Butt"*, ed. Gertrud Bauer Pickar (Munich: Fink, 1982), 43–50.

CHAPTER SEVEN

The Meeting in Telgte
(Das Treffen in Telgte)

THE MEETING IN TELGTE, AN OFFSHOOT OF *THE Flounder*, was a birthday present for and a tribute to Hans Werner Richter and the Group 47. Set three hundred years before 1947, in the last full year of the Thirty Years' War, *The Meeting in Telgte* is the fictionalized account of a meeting of war-weary German baroque poets, with a few publishers and other artists as guests, at an inn outside the small Westphalian town of Telgte.

Grass had carefully researched this era and these poets for the corresponding section of *The Flounder*. Now he projects onto their time the analogous concerns of the postwar and subsequent eras—the political factionalism and generational conflicts which racked the Group 47, as well as informal quarterly meetings of authors from East and West in which Grass regularly participated from 1973 to 1977.

Simon Dach is the wise, long-suffering analogue of Hans Werner Richter. The famous composer Heinrich Schütz puts in an appearance, as had the composer Hans Werner Henze at meetings of the Group 47. Georg Grefflinger seems to parallel Rudolf Augstein, founding publisher of the Hamburg weekly *Der Spiegel,* who was also an occasional guest at the meetings. (Grefflinger says he intends to leave Telgte for Hamburg to publish a weekly.) But who is the almost omniscient narrator? And who is Günter Grass, if anyone?

These questions cannot be answered with any certainty. The book is not simply a narration à clef. (And it inherits from *The Flounder* the fiction of reincarnation, of multiple simultaneous existences which would in any case cloud and complicate any simple allegorical relationships.) One of the poets, Georg Weckherlin, Milton's predecessor at the English court, has, like Grass, been involved in political matters, in the advising of heads of state. But it is for the swashbuckling Christoff Gelnhausen (a pseudonym for Hans Jakob Christoffel von Grimmelshausen) that Grass seems to have reserved the most sympathy, though the narrator specifically denies an identity with him.

He is the one who provides (stolen) goods to care for the poets' welfare and who often enough cuts through with his native wit the entangled knots of their philosophical disputes. He later becomes the author of *Der Abentheurliche Simplicissimus Teutsch* (1668), that remarkable fictional history of the Thirty Years' War.

He is also the creator of Mother Courage, a character later dramatized by Bertolt Brecht, who in Telgte is Libuschka, Gelnhausen-Grimmelshausen's consort, the earthy cook figure and owner of the inn. Students of baroque literature will no doubt wish to pursue the parallels between *Simplicissimus* and the historical treatment of World War II in the Danzig novels. Other matters may prove interesting as well, such as identifying the sources and the accuracy of the biographical details, the poems, the hymns, and the aphorisms cited.

For the general reader it may suffice to understand Grass's major point, expressed in the first line of the book: "Yesterday will be what tomorrow has been" (TT 7). Destroyed, divided, occupied by troops from all the major world powers, Germany, then, now, and in the future, is for the assembled writers still their fatherland. It is the home of their mother tongue, and the object of their affection as well as of their irritation. It is like the thistle symbolically placed in a pot next to the chair in which each poet sits in turn to read from his works, a noxious, thorny, and yet beautiful weed.

When the thistle is dropped on the floor, its pot shatters, but it remains upright, alive, and intact. So impressed are the wrangling authors at this, something they deem a miracle, that in an impulse of true patriotism they put aside their partisan differences and their ideological rancor and finally agree on the wording of a visionary, irenic manifesto. They address it to all the parties to the conflict. They call for a lasting peace, a restoration of the old order, yet one free from the seeds of new conflicts, from any restoration of old injustices.

Conscious of its great historic significance, they sign the document and proceed to the dining hall where a final communal meal of fish awaits them. As they praise their meal, compare it to the miracle of the fishes and the loaves and relate, of course, the tale of the speaking flounder, the inn catches fire and burns to the ground, destroying their manifesto.

That they then depart without making an attempt to reconstruct the document can be explained by the line: "Thus remained unsaid that which would not have been heard anyway" (TT 180). The implication, given the established set of parallels between past and present, is that such a document remains to be written. Perhaps now is the time, before someone burns the building, for all the writers, publishers, composers, and others from East and West to put aside their differences. Perhaps they could achieve a cultural unification. Then they could proclaim, for the sake of their poor divided fatherland and for the sake of the rest of the world whose troops are stationed there, a visionary manifesto of peace more than three hundred years overdue. Perhaps this time it would be heard, Grass seems to be saying.

CHAPTER EIGHT

Headbirths (Kopfgeburten)

HEADBIRTHS OR THE GERMANS ARE DYING OUT IS, AS the first word of the title implies, another offshoot of *The Flounder*. As a day-by-day account of an excursion, however, it is more closely related to *From the Diary of a Snail*, whose snail is evoked when Grass says she has already passed us several times. Also like the snail diary, *Headbirths* allows us rather intimate glimpses into Grass's personal life.

Here we learn more details, for example, about his early school novel "Die Kaschuben," and that it demonstrates, in Grass's view, how likely it is he would have been a Nazi if he had been ten years older. We learn how Grass views the stages of his own development, his writing about the "*Ver*gangenheit" (*pas*t), then the "*Gegen*wart" (pre*sent*), and the "Zu*kunft*" (fut*ure*) until finally he writes, he says, about the "Vergegenkunft" ("pasenture" [Kg 130]).

We learn more details of Grass's and other West German writers' readings with authors in East Berlin. We also learn that one of the participants, his friend Nicolas Born, died of cancer shortly after Grass's return from Asia.

Headbirths deals with the problems of world hunger and overpopulation, as *The Flounder* had, and it looks toward Asia, as had that section of *The Flounder* where the narrator poses as Vasco da Gama, a fictional reflection of Grass's trip to India in 1975.

Traveling under the auspices of the Goethe Institute, the Schlöndorffs show their films, and Grass reads a paper indebted to *The Meeting in Telgte*. The point of his presentation is that German writers in both East and West enjoy a great following and great respect. In a historic effort reaching back to the time of the Thirty Years' War, they have been able, perhaps more than any other Germans in East and West, to transcend their differences and make an attempt at a cultural reunification of their fatherland.

To follow him, Ute, and the Schlöndorffs on their journey back to the Orient, Grass creates a fictional couple, Harm and Dörte Peters. Former 1960s radicals both, now they are secondary school teachers of foreign languages and geography in Itzehoe, the town near which Grass's second home at Wewelsfleth is located. Grass decides to have the Peters travel with the Sisyphos Agency, an excuse for him to discuss this myth and to compare it to his and to Willy Brandt's tireless efforts to bring about progress, especially in the fight against world hunger. Their almost omniscient tour guide, Dr. Wenthien, provides further informed, albeit pessimistic, commentary on the problems of the Third World.

In this narrative, written in the style of a film script for Volker Schlöndorff, Harm and Dörte apply their professional knowledge of global population trends and their concern over the rape of the environment and the growing nuclear threat to the decision of whether or not to have a child. (Dörte has already had one abortion.) The overpopulation and squalor of slums in the Asian countries as well as the building of the Brokdorf nuclear power plant near their home in Itzehoe argue against an additional birth.

Primitive rituals associated with various mother goddesses they encounter, however, awaken deep maternal instincts in Dörte. Over Harm's rational objections she throws her birth-control pills into a bat-infested fertility shrine of a serpent goddess. Later it is Harm who yields to his paternal instincts and throws the pills into the toilet.

The matter is complicated by the xenophobic political speeches of the Bavarian Christian Socialist chancellor-candidate Franz Josef Strauss, a traditional bugbear for Grass. Strauss warns that the Germans are dying out, that Turks and other foreigners are taking over the country, and that Germans must increase their birthrate. (To Grass this is strongly reminiscent of Hitler's racist efforts in the same direction.) Fear soon spreads even to Harm and Dörte's students.

Standing in Shanghai surrounded by hordes of bicyclists, Grass tries to imagine various scenarios. What if the First and the Third Worlds were reversed? What if there were nearly a billion Germans and less than eighty million Chinese? Or, how does the Berlin Wall compare to the Great Wall of China and to the wall of death rays which would have to be built to keep the hungry masses from invading Europe? Or, how does German efficiency compare with Chinese efficiency? Could the Germans feed people as efficiently as they can make and sell weapons to kill them? (One important strand of the narrative concerns a liverwurst which Harm tries to deliver to an old school friend now living in Bali. He is a kind of personification of this deadly entrepreneurship, for he has apparently struck it rich smuggling weapons used in various armed conflicts in the region.)

The upshot of Grass's extended musings at the beginning of Orwell's decade, as he chooses to call it, is that Germany, and by extension the rest of the First World, *can* transcend nationalism and begin to exist on a global scale for the first time. Led perhaps in this effort by the authors, united perhaps under a National Endowment of German Culture envisioned by Willy Brandt and alluded to in the manifesto at the end of *The Meeting in Telgte*, Germans can turn from war and harness their efficiency to help fight world hunger. They can stop worrying about dying out and begin to prevent dying. They can stop worrying about having a child and begin to worry about children.

The last paragraph of the book is a symbolic cinematographic summary of the whole argument. Back home in Germany as they drive along in their well-preserved old Volkswagen, Harm and Dörte (*she* is in the driver's seat) almost hit a small Turkish boy who runs in front of their car. They manage to stop in time, and he and his friends, other Turkish boys, "celebrate with him his survival" (Kg 180).

And now, in a visionary scene, children stream out from all the neighboring streets and yards, all of them foreigners: Indian, Chinese, African, all happy

162

children. They increase and become numberless. They all celebrate with the little Turk who has been lucky once again. As the children cheerfully knock on the Volkswagen, the childless couple does not know what to say in German. But the very language Grass uses to describe their speechlessness is pidginized, pulled away from standard German in the direction of that of the children: "and not know what say in German." It is a subtle beginning away from nationalism and toward globalism, but it is a beginning.

CHAPTER NINE

The Rat
Die Rättin

AFTER THE APPEARANCE OF *HEADBIRTHS* IN 1980 GRASS
made a fact-finding trip to Nicaragua (1982). He
helped organize more meetings—in East Berlin
(1981), The Hague (1982), and West Berlin (1983)—
of writers from East and West to promote the cause
of peace. He participated in 1983 in a major conference at Saarbrücken on the future of Democratic
Socialism. And he made a speech at the Social Democratic admonitory commemoration of the fiftieth
anniversary of Hitler's rise to power on January 30,
1933. He published the collection *Aufsätze zur Literatur* (Essays on Literature) in 1980. Two large
volumes of graphic art accompanied by selected texts
from his writings called *Zeichnen und Schreiben*
(*Drawings and Words*) appeared in 1982 and 1984. A
volume of etchings and poems entitled *Ach Butt, dein
Märchen geht böse aus* (Alas, Flounder, Your Fairy
Tale Has an Unhappy Ending) was published in
1983, and a volume of political rebuttals entitled
Widerstand lernen (Learn to Resist) in 1984.

His graphic art was exhibited in well over a hundred galleries worldwide. These included the thema-
tic exhibits "Mit Sophie in die Pilze gegangen"
(Gathering Mushrooms With Sophie) staged by Gior-

gio Upiglio in Milan; "Als vom Butt nur die Gräte geblieben war" (When Only the Bones Remained of the Flounder) in the Galerie Andre of Berlin; and "Vatertag" (Father's Day) staged by Monika Beck of Hamburg. All included poems in their published portfolios or catalogues. An index of the etchings and lithographs, *In Kupfer, auf Stein* (In Copper, on Stone), appeared in 1986.

In 1982 Grass was awarded the Antonio Feltrinelli Prize, one of the most richly endowed cultural awards. (Other recipients include Thomas Mann, Igor Stravinsky, John Dos Passos, Henry Moore, Mies van der Rohe, and W. H. Auden.) In 1983 Grass was elected to a three-year term as president of the Berlin Academy of Arts.

His acceptance speech for the Feltrinelli Prize in Rome is entitled "Die Vernichtung der Menschheit hat begonnen" (The Annihilation of Humanity Has Begun). In it Grass says that literature, including all his previous works, even more than the other arts, always had one reliable ally: the future. Even though Brecht and Döblin were crushed by Nazism, Babel and Mandelstam by Stalinism, their works outlived these movements. Time was on their side. Now, Grass believes, the future is not so secure and cannot be presumed in the book he is writing.

The book referred to in this speech appeared in 1986. Written in large part during the Orwell year 1984, also the Chinese Year of the Rat, it is an anti-utopian nightmare entitled *Die Rättin* (*The Rat*). This book appears to imitate—in its intention to enlighten and to admonish human beings to do good by becoming truly good—that important work by Gotthold Ephraim Lessing entitled *Die Erziehung des Menschengeschlechts* (*The Education of the Human Race*) of 1780. (It makes frequent reference to this title.) It is informed with an air of eschatology and doomsday but also of irony and self-parody because it is something of a swan song for Günter Grass himself as he approaches age sixty. His previous works and their characters are here reunited and come full circle to their beginnings.

Oskar, whose blue eyes still see through every fraud, we are told, now reappears in time for *his* sixtieth birthday. "Is the time ripe for him once more?" (DR 29) asks the narrator, who is very nearly identical with Grass. Oskar Matzerath-Bronski, as he signs his name, can now almost hear the blackness of the Orwellian age growing. He is a collector of memorabilia and a specialist in the details of the era of *The Tin Drum*, the false fifties, as he calls them. Grass also makes him a film producer and, in an act of self-irony, an erstwhile producer of pornographic videos, whom the narrator engages to make a silent movie about acid rain and the death of the forests.

One of Oskar's favorite objects in his collection from the false fifties is a Braun record player made of white plastic with a plexiglass cover and hence popularly referred to as Snow White's casket. He still uses it to play the archetypal theme song of his fraudulent age, "The Great Pretender." Therefore, Oskar decides for this film on a parody of fairy tales and of the Walt Disney style: "The truth is named Donald Duck, and Mickey Mouse is his prophet!" (DR 87). Because it includes scarecrows, it is also reminiscent of Eddi Amsel.

166

He plans to bring together for this last, apocalyptic fairy tale all the figures from all the fairy tales to fight to save the forest from monied interests in league with corrupt church and government officials who are destroying it. The Brothers Grimm will play the role of environmentalist ministers of the interior in opposition to an almost allegorical chancellor, Helmuth Kohl. (The Grimms are based on members of Germany's ecologically oriented Green Party, who have been accused of living in the past, in a romantic, fairy-tale world.) The chancellor's own children, here called Hansel and Gretel (and who remind Oskar of Tulla and Störtebeker), will desert his cause for that of the environment. In the process they will expose his attempts to hide the truth about the death of the forest from his constituency: they cut down a large painted backdrop portraying a healthy forest for television cameras, revealing the silent, dead forest behind.

The magic "mirror, mirror, on the wall" will parallel Oskar's television screens. The witch with her amber eyes will distribute magic seeds to regenerate the earth and reclaim buildings, freeways, and airports for nature. She will also illuminate the human tendency to seek out and dehumanize scapegoats—Jews, rats, witches, Japs—and burn them. Red Riding Hood's grandmother will be on hand to read aloud from the Grimms' monumental German dictionary all permutations of the word *Angst*.

Meanwhile, Oskar's own grandmother—such is the linkage here between narratives—Anna Koljaiczek, still living in Poland, is approaching her 107th birthday. She extends an invitation to Oskar and to the other members of her far-flung family (of man), all related Kashubian characters from earlier Grass works, including the Colchics of Chicago. Apparently Joseph Koljaiczek did survive his swim under the raft of logs after all and was prevented only by his sudden death in 1945 from becoming a US Senator.

Precisely because of his grasp of the past it is also Oskar's gift to foresee the future. (Even his firm is called *Postfuturum*, yet another reference to Grass's idea of *Vergegenkunft* or "pasenture.") Therefore, Oskar manages the amazing feat of making a video of the coming event before he leaves Düsseldorf. He and his chauffeur, the former male nurse Bruno Münsterberg of *The Tin Drum*, load his Mercedes with this prophetic video. Other gifts include exactly 130 (apparently a multiple of the unlucky 13) plastic dwarves known as Smurfs, some playing red-and-white tin drums. They set out for Gdansk. There, among other things, Oskar will also pay a significant visit to the Polish Post Office, the site of the beginning of World War II.

Tightly interwoven with these strands of narrative, all of which function as potential scripts for Oskar's films, is an account of five women, including the narrator's wife, Damroka, an organist like Ute Grass and a transmogrification of Ulla Witzlaff of *The Flounder*. They "man" an ancient boat (launched in the significant year 1900) named *The New Ilsebill*. Ostensibly it sets out on a scientific expedition into the Baltic to study the link between pollution and the population explosion of jellyfish.

Along the way, however, their captain Damroka secretly consults with the flounder. (The others, in-

cluding the helmswoman, one of the three who originally caught him, have since bitterly dismissed his
ideas of a new humankind.) They are led by him to
Vineta, the site of a legendary sunken city. Closely
resembling Danzig but located off the mouth of the
Vistula, Vineta had once been ruled by women. But
it declined after 130 mysterious settlers from Hamelin on the Weser River arrived in 1284 and began to
oppose the matriarchy. Eventually the city was inun-
dated by a great storm.

The women pass the site near the German shore
where on May 3, 1945, British aircraft attacked
three ships, the *Cap Arcona*, the *Deutschland*, and
the *Thielbeck*. They were loaded with almost six
thousand inmates—Poles, Ukrainians, Jews, and
Germans—from the concentration camps at Neuen-
gamme and Stutthof. The oceanographer on *The New
Ilsebill* was, as a twelve-year-old, an eyewitness to
this horror. Now she recounts how those who survived the fires, explosions, and sinking and had managed, even in their weakened condition, to swim to
shore were shot one by one on the beach by SS men
and navy commandos.

Yet another strand of narrative/film script concerns a certain Lothar Malskat, a painter convicted
of art forgery in the fifties. He confessed to having
completely repainted the ceilings in Gothic buildings,
especially that of St. Mary's in Lübeck, rather than
having merely restored the (almost nonexistent) orig-
inals. Oskar labels the case "three master forgers,"
or the "triumvirate of forgers." It appeals to him because Malskat is, as Oskar had been, the *Zeitgeist* of
a corrupt age. He was the guilty, yet by comparison

almost innocent, microscopic victim of fraudulent behavior on the part of entrepreneurs and high church
and government officials eager to derive prestige and
income from the Gothic monument.

Malskat is thus the symbolic vehicle, as Oskar had
been, for bringing into focus the really great political
forgers of the age: Hitler's alter egos Walter Ulbricht
and Konrad Adenauer. These were the architects of a
fraudulent restoration of a militarized postwar Germany, now in two opposing halves, each beholden to
a larger, even more corrupt political "employer," the
Soviet Union and the United States respectively.

"The Great Pretender" should have become the
national anthem of both the German states, Oskar
maintains, albeit in the plural: "We are the Great
Pretenders." His film about Malskat and the false fifties, like Eddi Amsel's magic eyeglasses, will open
eyes, especially of young people, to the fraudulent
nature of the era and of its legacy, the final global
arms race.

The main strand of narrative concerns, as the title
implies, a rat, more precisely a she-rat, which the
narrator asks for and receives as a Christmas gift.
This barb is aimed at Franz Josef Strauss, who once
called writers like Grass "rats and blowflies." *Dog
Years*, of course, had dealt extensively with the rat
as a symbol for and simultaneously a victim of bes-
tialized humanity. The narrator also recalls Grass
had early on used two speaking rats in his play
"Flood" to comment on human calamity.

And now the she-rat does the same. While the narrator circles the earth in a space capsule, the she-rat
stands on a pile of human refuse, her nightmarish

speech modeled on that of the dead Christ from the
top of the world-building (from the novel *Siebenkäs*
of 1796 by the German author Jean Paul). She says
the human race is gone, only its refuse survives.
"Good riddance!", she says, to humans who were
"slave-holding slaves. Pious hypocrites! Exploiters!
. . . Nailed the only son of their God. Blessed their
weapons" (DR 32f)). As the rat relates the end, the
third stage of the three-stage World War, the Big
Bang, Ultimo, as she calls it, the narrator sees the
events happening before him on his video screen.

The rat begins her account well back in time with
the dinosaurs, who became extinct when rats learned
to crack open their enormous eggs, and with Noah's
flood, the first global calamity in which humans also
faced extinction. She explains that Noah had refused
to take rats on board his ark, so the rats saved themselves by digging deep tunnels and air chambers.
They stock them well with food, plug them tightly
with the bodies of elderly rats, and wait for the
floodwaters to subside. All their survival instincts
and heightened powers of perception stem from this
time, she says, hence rats unerringly know when to
leave a doomed ship.

Now, sensing the entire earth is doomed again, the
rats dig deep underground shelters. In anticipation,
some begin to make themselves immune to radioac-
tivity by tunneling under reactors and into radioac-
tive waste.

The rats, like the dying trees in the forest, try to
warn the humans their world is heading for calamity. Rats venture forth in large numbers in mute protest demonstrations—even the clouds appear to be

171

countless rats scurrying across the sky—as do other natural creatures such as the jellyfish, who sing an eerie *Kyrie* across the sea to lament the approaching end. Yet humans fail to realize what they are trying to say.

There are also cultural warning signs of imminent collapse, such as the phenomenon of punkers and other modern-day followers of various pied pipers. They adopt pet rats and dye them zinc green—a color Grass had previously used to identify young anarchists like Vero Lewand in *Local Anaesthetic*—to match their own dyed hair. Resembling nothing so much as the symbolic portraits of Oskar in the Art Academy in Düsseldorf, these are "children, permanently scared stiff, who made each other up with the pallor of death, who, full of presentiment, marked themselves with the green of corpses. Even their yellow, their orange were harmonized with mold and decay" (DR 46).

Soon, in a horrible reductio ad absurdum of Scherbaum's plan in *Local Anaesthetic*, mass immolations begin: "Wherever reason failed . . . the process was the same: Young people grouped themselves into a tight block . . . then the warning flash was ignited" (DR 72).

A certain "finalism" infects the entire race: the phrase "Auf Wiedersehen" (See you later) becomes extinct. Like the other natural creatures, these frightened children—a reincarnation of millenarian medieval flagellants—are crying out as well, but no one understands. They succeed only in frightening others and in making the "peace through strength" parties stronger.

172

The Orwellian punks and their rats are also linked
to 1984 because it is the six hundredth anniversary
of the legend of the *Rattenfänger* (rat catcher or pied
piper) of Hamelin in 1284. This provides Grass with
yet another strand of narrative—also explaining the
origins of those mysterious settlers in Vineta of
1284—one he thinks will especially interest Oskar.
Not only were there exactly 130 children led away
from the city by the piper but the piper's sirenic flute
is very similar to Oskar's sirenic drum.

Hitler is another in a long series of rat catchers
who have lead whole peoples to destruction. Oskar
views the matter of pipers and rats and Hitler in a
similar way, we are assured. He is someone who,
"like the harried creatures, sought refuge his whole
life long even when it occurred to him to pose as a
pied piper" (DR 60). The statement sheds considerable
light on Oskar's ambivalent nature: evil personified
and yet archetypal victim of evil.

The rat claims rats eventually gnawed their way
into the giant computers in East and West in which
doomsday was pre-programmed. Or perhaps it was
mice, she concedes, secretly planted in each enemy
computer by the KGB and the CIA, respectively. At
any rate, it was the humans who had pre-
programmed these computers and their missiles,
euphemistically called "peacemakers" and "friends of
the people." Any small, unexpected, but built-in
problem—for which rats and mice are mere
metaphorical scapegoats—could have set them off.

Ultimo occurs at noon on a Sunday. The five
women on *The New Ilsebill* are preparing to descend
into the underwater queendom which they will call

173

Feminal City: prophetically they suddenly see the streets swarming with rats. Oskar's video just reaches the end, where it shows the birthday guests watching the video of the birthday party, whose guests are watching a video of the party.

The women and the wooden superstructure of their boat are vaporized. The steel hull drifts aimlessly across the Baltic. Oskar seeks refuge under the skirts of his grandmother. But he and all the birthday guests are desiccated, reduced to shriveled gnomes by the enhanced radiation of the low-blast neutron weapons called "friends of the arts" with which Gdansk, an artistic landmark, was targeted. Only the already shriveled 107-year old Anna Koljaiczek survives, blinded by the flash of the bomb and kept alive on purée of young rat by the rats, themselves now zinc green from the radiation.

When she eventually dies, her mummy, along with that of Oskar, found under her skirts and taken for that of a newborn (his return to the womb thus grotesquely accomplished), is not eaten as all the others are. (The final fate of humanity, like Lena Stubbe at Stutthof in *The Flounder*, is to be food for rats.) Instead it is moved to Gdansk along with many of the birthday gifts and placed on the altar of St. Mary's Church. Here she becomes a kind of fertility goddess to the hungry rats, a grotesque new Virgin with Oskar as the Child, the role he played in this very church with the Dusters. A wrought-iron sign reading "Solidarity," a gift of the Bronskis, workers at the Lenin shipyards, stands nearby.

In a kind of crèche scene the Smurfs are assembled

about this new Virgin. When one of her fingers
breaks off, it seems to point at a group of Smurfs
who are tilling the soil. Since they have not yet begun to imitate the religious discord of the humans
(eventually, in a war of religion, 130 rats will be cru-
cified on a hill outside town), the rats take this as a
sign. They begin to plant and harvest. They subdue
mutant pests such as the mammalian blowflies (!)
and the flying snails (!), and soon they live in abun-
dance. Later, having become somewhat more secular-
ized, they open a museum of human history complete
with models of concentration camps, a tin drum, and
the Solidarity sign.

But there is another element in this nightmare.
Shortly before they are vaporized, the five women
dock *The New Ilsebill* at Visby on the Swedish island
of Gotland and go ashore for the afternoon. There
they join a group protesting the use of animals in
medical research. They follow the crowd to a building
on the outskirts of town. Rocks are thrown—some of
these protesters are the same violent women who
tried to stone the flounder—and glass is shattered.
The animals escape. The women return to their boat
and cast off in haste before the police arrive, but
they have left the boat unlocked.

Now, from his vantage point in orbit, a helpless
human god to the rats, the narrator watches the
hulk of *The New Ilsebill* moving under its own power
into the harbor of Gdansk, again called Danzig.
When it docks, strange stowaways emerge: human-
rats or rathumans are on board, a product of gene
manipulations in the laboratory at Visby. (Visby is a

branch of the University of Uppsala, where—the narrator now recalls—genetic material from Egyptian mummies had been successfully cloned.)

Called Manippels, they are also known to the rats as Watsoncricks after the discoverers of DNA. They are blond, blue-eyed, hominoid dwarves, about the size of a three-year-old boy. They have the heads of rats and three fingers on each hand like the Smurfs, whose language they speak. (The mummies link them to Oskar's grandmother. They are also linked to the punks and to the pied piper by the strange story of a maid of Hamelin—Gret—who is impregnated by her pet rat—Hans—and bears a litter of thirteenth-century rathumans.)

The rats suspect they have some swinish genes as well, for their tails are those of pigs. The females tend to dominate. Programmed to start with no history and with no values, like Eddi Amsel's scarecrows, these monsters retrace the stages of human development: they reinvent fire, drink beer, and march in formation. Like the Goths (also from Gotland) and Swedish soldiers of the Thirty Years' War before them, they gradually conquer the entire area.

Naturally these new hominoids begin to exploit and consume the rats and to build concentration camps for them. Strengthened by having put behind them their national and their religious differences, however, and united under the sign of Solidarity, taken from the museum as their banner, the rats finally eradicate this last monstrous creation of the human race. Unlike the humans and their monstrosities, the rats survive because they have learned how to change and have learned how to cooperate.

As in Jean Paul's story, in the end the tale of the rat is only a dream with the peculiar optical properties of a dream. Oskar returns safely from Gdansk, having suffered nothing worse than a minor traffic accident, the theft of his Mercedes hood ornament, and an attack of prostatism requiring catheterization. Damroka writes about an awful American horror film she saw in Visby with monsters, half human, half animal. Then she returns home safe and sound, complaining about the women's inability to get along with each other. Everyone, including Volker Schlöndorff, attends Oskar's sixtieth birthday party. During the party news arrives that Anna Koljaiczek has died of natural causes.

Oskar has begun to make the story of the rathumans into a film entitled "Davor und Danach" (Before That and After That), a completive sequel to Grass's play *Davor*. The film about Malskat and the one about the fairy-tale figures and the dying forest are postponed. (The latter is to end with the flight of the Brothers Grimm back into the past and the total destruction—by monstrous military machines à la "Star Wars"—of the forest and the ecological "romantics" who try to save it.) Until he jumps out at the end and plays the innocent child, Oskar will be in one of these machines along with the industrial bosses and the corrupt politicians and priests who bless the weapons: he has been accustomed from his youth, we read, to be involved with violence.

177

But for now, even if it has to learn these lessons from rats or at least from *Die Rättin*, humanity has a second chance to develop a sense of community, a sense of charity, of loving and of feeding one's neighbor. It was all just a bad dream. (Or was it?)

In the end the narrator dreams there may be at least a glimmer of hope after all that humans can act humane. Though the rats laugh at this hope, in a kind of inchoate stammer he perseveres: "But I want to, to try again to . . . Just assuming we humans did still exist . . . this time we really want to be for each other and peace-loving besides, do you hear, in love and gentle, as we are created by nature" (DR 505). "A beautiful dream," replies the rat before she disappears.

INTERIM CONCLUSION

REVIEWING THE SCOPE OF GRASS'S *OEUVRE* FROM THE vantage point of this culminating tale, it is clear that the artist has portrayed with remarkable consistency for over three decades what he sees through his peculiar optics as the most dangerous insanities of our age. Yet out of it all, he has synthesized some very reasonable prescriptions for a sane and peaceful world.

He knows these prescriptions are probably futile. He knows he is a dreamer. He knows the chances for doomsday are increasing. He has seen his snails stopped in their tracks. Perhaps there will be no future. But he does not give up. Even his predictions of calamity are valiant attempts to avert calamity.

If there is a future, one can be sure a tireless Günter Grass will be there, working to extend and to humanize it, writing, drawing, etching, sculpting, lecturing, campaigning, and cooking up ideas in his own controversial and inimitable way.

CHAPTER TEN

The Plays and Poems in Retrospect

TO PLACE A DISCUSSION OF THE PLAYS AND RELATED poems of Günter Grass *after* that of his prose fiction is to trace his own creative process in reverse. Yet, because Grass's symbol systems have remained essentially consistent for over three decades, this reversal has much to recommend it. For an initial understanding of Grass it allows the reader to bring to these relatively more cryptic stages of Grass's artistic inquiry the full range of theme, imagery, and technique derived from his larger, more fully developed fictional corpus.

"Flood"

His first play, "Flood" (1957), is a case in point. A dramatic elaboration in two acts of a poem bearing the same title in the collection *Die Vorzüge der Windhühner* of 1956, "Flood" is so perplexing it has been categorized by puzzled critics as theater of the absurd. Yet it is no more difficult to understand than certain portions of Grass's fiction if these were taken out of their narrative contexts and made to stand alone on stage. Read ex post facto against the larger context of Grass's entire oeuvre, while retaining some opaque references, perhaps to imagery which has not (yet) been further developed, "Flood" nevertheless yields up a good deal of meaning.

The flood of the title itself can be better understood, for example, in connection with the floods of the Vistula at the beginning of *Dog Years*. There the mythical river of time washes down to the historian/artist Eddi Amsel the flotsam of previous wars and other violent calamities. These range from the murder of Adalbert of Prague by Mestwin's daughter—in *Dog Years* the murder weapon is the traditional ax, not an iron spoon as in *The Flounder*—to the Napoleonic occupation of Danzig under Rapp. That the flood of the play is a symbol of a similar and perhaps more recent military calamity is underscored by the presence on stage of anthropomorphic rats. These are played by actors wearing large grotesque rat masks, who compare the current situation to that in Paris in 1871, when during the Franco-Prussian War rats were eaten by starving humans.

It is the *female* rat, Pearl, as in *The Rat* and as predicted by the tendency of *The Flounder*, who is the most perceptive, and the most fearful, about the consequences of the flood. This is in part because she has also suffered the most during wartime at the hands of humans. We learn from an account of her nightmares that her entire family has been exterminated by a military doctor with a white smock and a hypodermic syringe. He bears a strong resemblance to those infamous concentration-camp physicians like Josef Mengele.

Even after the rain stops and the floodwaters begin to recede, it is the rats, perennial Grassian symbols of global catastrophe, who realize that a return to business as usual will only lead to further, then final, calamity. So the rats plan a postwar pilgrimage to Hamelin. (*The Rat* has no doubt correctly conditioned us to see, ex post facto, in this march a kind of mute memento mori for the doomed human race.) The humans, on the other hand, who lack an eye, the rats believe, for the nuances of natural phenomena and any feeling at all for symbolism, foolishly look to the romantic rainbow as a symbol of hope. They long for the appearance of a dove with a bit of green in its beak as a symbol of permanent peace, without themselves seeking to ensure no further floods come upon them.

The human beings in "Flood," the symbolic human family, include the patriarch Noah, like Amsel a collector of historical trivia such as candelabra and inkwells, including one used by Queen Luise of Prussia (presumably during her stay in the Matern's mill). His sister-in-law is Betty, for whom, not unlike Oskar, the past is still alive in the form of pictures in her "holy" photo album.

Noah's daughter Yetta is a clear forerunner (with the hindsight gained from the prose fiction) of Vero Lewand and other violent females like Tulla. Yetta also used to play doctor and nurse with Nuchi and Axel, we learn. Because of the ardent lover it has washed up like a drowning cat to her bed, Yetta wishes fervently in the last lines of the play that another flood might come, as high, perhaps even higher, than the last one.

Her previous boyfriend is Henry, who insists there will be a future. He indulges in fantasies of sun-drenched days to come, such as those he once experienced in Florence, where even dove-droppings—another misleading symbol of future peace—seemed to glisten like precious mother-of-pearl.

The violent Leo is Noah's wayward son, who magically materializes from a crate containing photo albums. He is evoked when his aunt Betty shows his father a picture of him. He wears clothing resembling a uniform and brings with him the smell and climate of the jungle. He has been in Tonkin, Saigon, and in Laos, we are told. His likewise uniformed friend is Kongo, a former boxer living by the military motto *Durchhalten* (fight-to-the-finish) like Field Marshall Schörner from *Local Anaesthetic*. As a kind of personification of brute, libidinal force, he immediately proceeds to make love to Yetta.

It was Kongo who originally convinced Leo to leave his home and go into the Rhineland. This is the apparent starting point of Leo's global military career, which with its odor of Dien Bien Phu and of Korea appears to have most recently spread to Asia. It echoes one of Hitler's first major military moves against the treaties of Versailles and Locarno: the unopposed remilitarization of the Rhineland on March 7, 1936. In euphemisms pregnant with military meaning, Noah and Kongo rehearse the past:

Noah   "Weren't you the gentleman who once succeeded in convincing my son to go into the Rhineland, and from there, you surely already know what I mean.

Kongo   Exactly right, that was me. You mean, un-
less I'm very much mistaken, that little
Sunday excursion. Just lasted a little longer than planned. (Ts 19).

The (tropical) rains have brought the brutal soldiers Leo and Kongo, the darkly irrational forces of
war, out of their Pandora's box. Their journey takes
them onward, along a logical continuum from light
to dark, from hot to cold, from the rain age to the Ice
Age, from the tropics via Europe to the North Pole,
from world war to the global extinction of life.

Leo attempts to explain this logic, the logic of his
attraction to ice, by relating a strange story about
his erotic fantasy involving a trapeze artist. Her
well-illuminated legs high above him in the circus
tent appeared to him first to be of porcelain. Then
they looked like two columns of ice leading to her
pubis, to a little temple in the Arctic, as Leo tells the
tale, to her North Pole, which is closed to every expedition. At the conclusion of her act, to the accompaniment of firecracker-like applause, as she glides
down a rope, Leo says she melts and flows down, revealing her dirty, ugly skin and her smile like a pud-
dle of horse piss.

To underscore the meaning of his story Leo drops a
crystal bowl on the floor. This has the effect, in Leo's
mind, of ending the clapping and the melting, of
spreading the North Pole like bits of ice over all the
world: "Just this sound, this result, the North Pole
spread all around. Arctic from the Niger to Heidel-
berg, but no applause" (Ts 31f).

At first viewing, the episode may appear completely absurd. But we have identified numerous links in such works as *The Tin Drum*, *Cat and Mouse*, and *Local Anaesthetic* between broken glass, the Crystal Night, pathological sexual fantasies, and the conduct of aggressive war. To one familiar with Grass's oeuvre, then, the association between Leo's sexual impotence, the warlike shattering of crystal, and the inexorable spread of the Ice Age to the entire world makes rather good symbolic sense.

We learn further that Leo plans to take with him to the North Pole the broken grandfather clock, to prevent the others from having it repaired. A further note of finality is thus added to the apocalypse when Kongo asks: "But what shall the people do without the big hand and the little hand and without the little minutes in between that are necessary for life" (Ts 56).

By taking away the clock and its vital contents, that is, time, the evil Leo, with the strong encouragement of his anarchist sister Yetta, presages the end of time. This is the destruction of time in a frozen postwar wasteland like that in *The Rat*, where the shattered clock on Anna Koljaiczek's wall marks the exact moment of Ultimo.

The poem "Flood" also contains a corroborating image combining clocks and the end of life:

Often we stand before the water gauge
and compare our concerns like clocks.
Some of them can be reset.
But when the containers overflow, the inherited measure is full,
we shall have to pray (GG 25).

185

And at the end of act 1, when Noah speaks as a biblical prophet—"What have ye made of my house. Ye fill it with infamy, with filth, higher than the water" (Ts 41))—he reads the account of the biblical flood, the end of all flesh, from a black book.

Here the religious imagery and the overflowing containers of the poem are echoed, and even the final stage direction functions as an apocalyptic coda: "There, there: That same day were all the fountains of the great deep broken up and the windows of heaven were opened. *Slowly it gets dark*" (Ts 42; see Genesis 7:11).

"Mister, Mister"

Grass's second play, "Mister, Mister," premiered in 1958. Only slightly less surrealistic than "Flood," it involves a systematic serial murderer named Bollin. During the course of the play itself Bollin proves to be singularly inept. He succeeds in killing no one, and in the end is himself killed by his own revolver, which he has foolishly lent to a pair of persistent juveniles, Sprat, a thirteen-year-old girl, and Slick, a fourteen-year-old boy.

Bollin first encounters Sprat and Slick in the prologue to act 1 when the children come by on roller skates and discover him sitting on a park bench. He offers them candy, but they want to see what he has in his pocket. They meet again in act 2 in a forest where Bollin has trapped a forest ranger in a pit and is in the process of burying him alive. The children distract Bollin and go off with the forest ranger, who lectures them on the difference between pine and spruce. Finally, then, at the end of act 4, Sprat and Slick appear again, and repeatedly ask Bollin if he doesn't have a "thingamajig" in his pocket. They make off with his watch, fountain pen, then finally his revolver, with which Bollin is killed.

In the meantime Bollin attempts to rape and murder a young girl named Sophie, who is sick in bed with influenza. (This portion of "Mister, Mister" is identical with the one-act play entitled "Die Grippe" [Influenza], published separately in 1957.) He suddenly jumps out from under her bed, where he has been hiding. And though the sight of Bollin also immediately suggests to her mind the word *Zuchthaus* (penitentiary), one of those for which she had been searching for her crossword, Sophie calmly continues to work on the puzzle.

Her widowed mother is likewise unruffled at the sight of Bollin (an eligible bachelor after all), and invites him to return on Sunday for her son's third birthday celebration. When Bollin departs she kindly reminds him to take his "thingamajig," his revolver, which he has left on a table. He grabs the gun and Sophie's doll Pinkie as well, which is lying nearby.

At the beginning of act 2 Bollin is seen playing a sadomasochistic game with Pinkie. Pretending to act at her request, he first stabs her in the belly with a knife, then he sews up the slit before all the sawdust can leak out. Next, he hangs her on a hook suspended from the ceiling. Imitating a soldier on a military firing range complete with an imaginary marksmanship instructor, he shoots at her with an air pistol. When she is facing him he misses three times because she looks at him cross-eyed, but when he turns her around he easily scores three hits.

This bizarre activity has echoes in at least two poems. "Lamento bei Glatteis" (Lamentation at the Sight of Black Ice), from *Die Vorzüge der Wind-hühner,* describes sawdust from inside the doll Sanna being strewn because there is black ice outside (the slit through which it leaks out is called her vulva). The twelfth stanza of "Aus dem Alltag der Puppe Nana" (Everyday Occurrences in the Life of the Doll Nana), which first appeared in *Akzente* in 1956, is entitled "Schlechte Schützen" (Bad Marksmen) and reads:

> The doll was nailed to a board
> and arrows thrown at her.
> But no arrow hit her,
> because the doll looked cross-eyed.

The erotic overtones of the scene in the play, reinforced by the reference to the vulva in the poem, suggest we begin to view Bollin with his phallic knife and military gun as another of those impotent Grassian antiheroes. He is another heir to Adolf Hitler, related to Oskar and Pilenz, but more specifically akin to Matern and to Starusch (Sprat and Slick also happen to think Bollin has a toothache, we learn in passing). Both of them also behave like impotent serial killers attempting to wreak revenge with their phallic weapons on various wives, daughters, and girlfriends.

In one of Starusch's murderous fantasies, having become like Bollin a systematic cat-burglar, he kills his fiancée, a famous opera singer, by taking her picture and publishing it in a magazine. This is exactly paralleled, though partially inverted, in "Mister, Mister": Bollin's next "victim" after Sophie, Pinkie, the forest ranger, and a barber who gives him a ticket to "The Barber of Seville" is the singer Mimi Landella. Called Diva for short, she is a publicity seeker with a photographer boyfriend who feels honored to be the latest in a long line of opera stars murdered by the famous Bollin, and to have the event captured on film.

In the end, limping like Walter Matern, Bollin is shot by Sprat. She then suggests a game to Slick. He can threaten her with the gun, rape her, just as in a case she has read about in the newspaper—though she thinks this somehow involves her navel—they can have a baby and get married. They skip away singing their song:

> Mister, Mister, aintcha, aintcha
> aintcha, aintcha got
> any little thingamajig
> maybe in yer pocket(Ts 120).

Grass links the children's lack of sexual sophistication with their inability or unwillingness to recognize and learn to avoid a pathological killer like Bollin. This is reflected in their euphemistic reference to the murder weapon as a thingamajig. Sophie and her hopeful mother share in the same dangerous innocence, real or pretended, which this once ends happily for them.

Diva, on the other hand, knows Bollin is a killer—she has her debut after Bollin kills the prima donna

to whom she is the understudy—but her desire for
publicity and stardom make her cooperate with him.
The forest ranger, too, knows Bollin is dangerous.
Bollin has killed all his associates. But even though
he is armed and capable of arresting Bollin, he
allows Bollin to escape when he immediately reim-
merses himself in his narrow, specialized occupation
and goes off lecturing the children on the subject of
trees.

Each member of the society, then, for varying
reasons, refuses to recognize or to confront Bollin and
his deadly aggressions, the systematic pathological
perversions of his sexual drives. Even his death is
only accidental and solves nothing, since the children, the Tulla and Störtebeker figures of the play,
now become the heirs both to his weapon and to his
role as rapist and murderer. Surely his legacy, like
that of Adolf Hitler, until it is fully addressed and
looked fully in the face by society—the implication of
the Pinkie episode is that he would be incapable of
doing her any harm if she faced him, if she even
looked at him cross-eyed—will yet cause much harm.

"Only Ten Minutes to Buffalo"

"Only Ten Minutes to Buffalo" is a one-act play
which first appeared in *Akzente* in 1958. The scene is
a flowery meadow with grazing cows, in the middle
of which a rusted old steam locomotive stands, over-
grown with vegetation. An artist, Kotschenreuther,
sits at his easel painting a seascape with a sailing

ship, a frigate, to be exact. This causes the rustic cowherd Axel to express his bewilderment: he quite naturally expects Kotschenreuther to be painting a landscape with cows.

In nautical terminology Kotschenreuther then somewhat paternalistically explains that Axel needs to throw these stupid titles—cows, ships—overboard and begin to perceive the world through what he calls new aspects, sensitive instruments, clairaudient mechanisms. He then asks Axel for a glass of sail juice, by which he means milk, Axel ascertains, for he stipulates it must be white, like Moby-Dick.

With this unmistakable invitation ringing in our ears to view the play—and perhaps all of Grass—in such symbolic terms, we next see the engineer Krudewil and his fireman Pempelfort pretending they are racing through the landscape in the old locomotive. Their destination appears to be Buffalo, which they plan to reach in thirty, then twenty, then ten minutes.

The nautical imagery of the painting is reinforced by the revelation that Krudewil and Pempelfort are really sailors after all. They have deserted the navy, their ship—which was a frigate, as it happens—and their captain, a woman curiously named Fregatte (Frigate) as well. From her Krudewil has also stolen a pistol. As they pretend to steam along, these sailors even convert their speed to nautical miles, and when they stop to refuel—with pats of dried cow dung—they refer to it as lying at anchor.

Eventually they are forced to halt because they see someone on the tracks. When they investigate, they discover it is none other than Fregatte, their former captain. She is flying all her flags and, in an image reminiscent of ships' stacks, smoking three cigars. In fear of her wrath Krudewil hides the pistol in the smokestack of the locomotive. After a ritual litany the two sailors go off with Fregatte (who is dressed in an admiral's uniform, carrying a telescope, and wearing a model frigate as a hat) to harpoon Moby-Dick.

From the cowherd Axel's point of view, of course, they are merely chasing cows about the meadow. In the end Alex and his dog Jonah—yet another echo of whales—climb into the locomotive and drive it slowly off stage as Krudewil's pistol hidden in the smokestack becomes overheated and explodes.

Though the sheer lunacy of the situation itself has an undeniable appeal, Grass's other works suggest several possible avenues to a deeper understanding of the piece. One is based on an essay from *Akzente* of 1957 entitled "Der Inhalt als Widerstand: Bausteine zur Poetik" (Content as Resistance: Building Blocks of Poetics), the core of which is formed by a dialogue between none other than Pempelfort and Krudewil. Here they are two poets who walk through a meadow filled with flowers, exactly like that in the play, while discussing the process of making poems.

Their inclusion in this essay has suggested to some critics that "Only Ten Minutes to Buffalo" can be read as a study in epistemological aesthetics: how does the artist depict reality and arrive at truth? Does the artist Kotschenreuther, for example, reveal the truth of the nautical background of Krudewil and Pempelfort by painting a surrealistic ship in place of realistic cows? Or does the naive Axel best cut through pretension simply by taking the locomotive for a locomotive and driving off in it while all the others in the piece chase illusions? Or, paradoxically, can both be possible?

Basing our judgment on artist figures such as Oskar and especially Eddi Amsel, we can say both are possible. Grass seems committed to the paradox that art, in itself an illusory medium, can cut through illusions and delusions to reveal the true reality hidden below. In this sense "Only Ten Minutes to Buffalo," like the other plays and poems, is a surrealistic invitation to look at the reality beyond illusion. It invites us to call a gun a gun, not a thingamajig, as in "Mister, Mister," or to call a war a war, not a little Sunday excursion, as in "Flood."

The figure of Fregatte, too, is such just a surrealistic artistic peephole to reality, an important clue to which, retroactively recognizable from *The Tin Drum*, is her reference to herself as a wooden figurehead. The reference comes in a lengthy speech in which Fregatte seems to be tracing the history of her life.

Originally an innocent Flemish virgin, she says, in a century when witchcraft and hexing were popular pastimes, she was bewitched and changed into a wooden figurehead. After some pirate voyages and sea battles she was kissed by a leaping dolphin, the spell was broken, and she became an admiral. Immediately thereafter Lepanto, Trafalgar, and Aboukir (all sites of great naval battles) are mentioned. She was victorious, and was sunk, she continues, and became that sea serpent "which sweetened the sour-pickle era [a time of hardship, of bitter rations, translated summer doldrums] for newspaper readers" (Ts 147).

A rereading of the Niobe chapter in *The Tin Drum* reveals that most of the elements of Fregatte's bizarre life exactly parallel events associated with Niobe, that man- and boy-killing figurehead, the personification of war and destruction, whose essence informs the Crystal Night and the Heavenly Gasman. The statue was originally modeled after a *Flemish maiden* we read, an innocent person near and dear to the merchant who had commissioned the work. Soon thereafter she is accused of *witchcraft* and burned. The figurehead itself is captured by the semi-official Danzig *pirates* Paul Beneke and Martin Bardewiek, and after their demise sails with the Danzig fleet under Eberhard Ferber in his unsuccessful *sea battles* against Denmark.

Mutinies break out unexpectedly, and religious wars, attacks by Swedish troops, as well as countless other deaths and calamities are linked to her presence in the city. When Herbert, accompanied by Oskar, takes the job as a museum guard for Niobe, ostensibly to prove she is harmless they stage a mock rehearsal of her career: under the *models of frigates* and other warships suspended from the ceiling Herbert dresses up as an *admiral* bearing a *telescope*. Oskar dresses as the admiral's page; together they play *Trafalgar*, and scatter Napoleon's fleet at *Aboukir*.

Such additional illumination of the Niobe image from *The Tin Drum* should suffice to make it clear that Fregatte is a maritime female counterpart of someone like Kongo in "Flood," a personification of the history of war. In that light, even such an opaque image, not directly referred to in other works, as that of her being sunk and becoming a sea serpent which then sweetens the sour-pickle time for newspaper readers, might be now rather transparently explainable. It appears to be an allegory of German submarine warfare during those times—in both World Wars—when the Allies controlled the surface of the seas and whose successes sweetened the bad news a bit for Germans reading accounts of the war in newspapers.

Be that as it may, here Fregatte has again taken command of her mutinous *Volk*, and has set off once more on her monomaniacal and suicidal hunt for the elusive and deadly white whale of military conquest. The final event of the play is the explosion of Fregatte's pistol—Axel and the train are thus also drawn into the madness—an audible echo of her military assault on Moby-Dick, the inevitable continuation of her long history of violence and destruction.

"The Wicked Cooks"

Grass's fourth play, "The Wicked Cooks," premiered in 1961. At a full five acts it exceeds all the earlier plays in length, in complexity, and—if that were possible—in the perplexity in which it has left viewers, readers, and critics.

As the play opens, a group of cooks is summoned by their leader, Chef Petri, who blows on a trumpet—the image is identical to that in the poem

"Blechmusik ("Music for Brass") from *Die Vorzüge der Windhühner*—and informs them they face ruin. A certain mysterious person called the Count posses- ses the recipe for a special gray soup, which he calls November soup, the soup of the phoenix, and the gray eminence. It could put the cooks out of business because all their customers now insist on ordering this soup and this soup only.

Chef Petri and a group of rival cooks under Chef Kletterer spend five acts attempting to get the rec- ipe. In the end the Count commits suicide with his girlfriend, one of the cooks runs away with the rec- ipe, and a foot race ensues.

But what does the soup mean? A careful—and un- daunted—reader of Günter Grass may hope to discov- er the recipe for this rich symbolic mulligan by mak- ing an inventory of related elements in other works, whose symbolic values are more or less understood, and then applying these, in part retroactively, to the play.

We have seen from the final pages of *The Tin Drum*, for example, that it was the Black Cook who cast her evil political and martial shadow over all the events of Oskar's young life, even when Axel and Nuchi cooked their repulsive soup and forced him to eat it with a spoon. This image is an exact duplicate of one in the play when the wicked cooks threaten the Count with some of their soup, a lethal, metal- laden "truth serum."

Grass's graphic cooks are invariably menacing, like those in the collage of thirteen menacing cooks on a gory photograph of severed fish heads in blood- stained newspaper of 1958 (Me 36f), a symbol of our

bloodstained age. They always loom large and powerful, wielding weapons such as the knife used to
slaughter a chicken (ZS I 79)—an image also found in
the play—or, most often, a raised cooking spoon (Me
39).

Their cooking spoon is also an instrument of violence, we learn, like that with which her grandmother terrorized Lorchen Matern. This was immor-
talized by Eddi Amsel in a sculpture/scarecrow
which, next to his Great Cuckoo Bird, was the most
frightening to man and beast of his entire produc-
tion. In the hands of Mestwina, of course, the cooking
spoon becomes the first murder weapon, an exact inversion of its original life-sustaining purpose.

The cooks leaping over a wall into the Count's garden recalls the scene in *Dog Years* where nine
masked SA men leap into Eddi Amsel's garden, a
scene itself artistically redepicted in the scarecrow
ballet. There the garden is the world, trampled down
and destroyed in the end by a monstrosity that antic-
ipates those in the apocalyptic fairy-tale film of *The
Rat*.

In "The Wicked Cooks" the Count says the cooks
sit on his wall like "ravens that turned out somewhat too pale" (Ts 222). This recalls those other black
birds, crows, involved in the assault on Jenny and
Eddi as well as in the rape-murder in *The Flounder*.
And when they jump down into the garden, the
Count utters the apocalyptic statement: "Now they're
stamping everything to bits!" (Ts 223).

References to birds, and the overall dancelike nature of the play, based as it is on the ballet "Five
Cooks," forge even more links to the symbology of

the scarecrow ballet, as does the cooks' robotlike language. This sheds further light on the question of color symbolism. In the play, as if to underscore their paradoxical affinity to the Black Cook, the cooks always appear in their ghostly garb against a sinister black background. They appear against the night, for example, under a black canopy, in the service of customers in black suits, in parallel to black chimney sweeps, or portrayed as pale ravens.

This is an exact, albeit inverted, restatement of the black and white contrasts informing *Dog Years*, such as the black crows in the white snow which remind Brauxel so painfully of the wintry scene in the garden and near the black Gutenberg monument. It reminds one as well of the white mountain of bones and the black rats and crows at the antiaircraft battery.

In *The Tin Drum* it involves the white gulls, the black eels and black horse's head. Oskar's fixation on white nurses' uniforms, the black of nuns' habits and of the Black Cook comes to mind, as does the triangular black shape of Luzie Rennwand's face and of the Nazi pennant. All of these are amalgamated in the long poem "Zauberei mit den Bräuten Christi" (Magical Tricks with the Brides of Christ) from *Gleisdreieck*, the last image of which is that of an armada of windblown nuns meeting Nelson at Trafalgar. This image is also recognizable as that so profitably painted by Lankes.

In the play all these blend into the gray of the Count's soup and into the gray of his wall, which he has partially covered with white paint. Grass's inversion of black and white suggests—as it also does in the poem "Köche und Löffel" ("Chefs and Spoons") from *Gleisdreieck*—that these evil characters cannot deny their black background even when they dress in white. They are black purveyors of death even as they pretend to be white purveyors of life.

In the emerging political and historical pattern thus recognized, the techniques used to get the recipe out of the Count resemble nothing so much as those employed by governments to obtain intelligence information. Here are nocturnal meetings in odd places, threats of coercion, the use of "truth serum," and blackmail involving the Count's potentially embarrassing sexual preferences and practices. We encounter bribery with money and with sexual favors, as well as the use of double agents. And the euphemistic jargon used by Petri sounds for all the world like that employed by intelligence agencies.

In this light certain other bits of this "absurd" play seem to fall into place, including the competitive nature of the two groups of cooks. When Kletterer greets Petri with an inquiry about his stock portfolio, for example, we realize that in its well-appointed kitchen—serving men with black suits and blonde women—Petri's cooks seem to represent the capitalistic West. Kletterer's masses, on the other hand, with their roots in the proletarian world of the "*Volks*küchen" or "*Gross*- und *Betrieb*sküchen" (which smack of the East German term for a collective enterprise: *Volkseigener Betrieb*), represent the communistic East.

The names suggested by the Count for the gray soup hint at related matters. November soup, though it could simply be a reference to the dismal weather of that month, also reminds a German reader of the violent events of November 1918, of the incomplete revolution that gave birth to the ill-fated Weimar Republic. Phoenix soup smacks of the postwar world rising out of the ashes, especially since the phoenix is an image also used by Grass in *Dog Years* and at the end of "Flood" to refer to the postwar era. Gray eminence, a term referring to a person who wields secret power, might also suggest some sort of continuing secret political struggle.

The cooks say that their future—and that of the human race, the Count adds—is dependent upon the soup. This reflects its use here as a symbol of that for which both great postwar powers, and both their microscopic puppet states, the two Germanies, strive: any secrets, especially nuclear secrets, that might lead to military superiority.

It is surely no coincidence that "The Wicked Cooks" was written during the critical cold-war period when the Adenauer administration agreed to allow its NATO ally, the United States, to arm the *Bundeswehr* with atomic weapons. Similar nuclear deployments in East Germany were made by the Soviet Union under the Warsaw Pact. Seen in this way, the *foot* race at the end of the play, when one of the cooks becomes the heir to the Count's secret, can be seen as an *arms* race. It takes on a momentum of its own, causing the cooks to run for the sake of running, even if it must be in bare feet, they explain, just as governments feverishly pursue weapons systems which, as spoons do the cooks, corrupt and at the same time impoverish them.

It may not be going too far to see in the Count a

kind of Hitler figure. He is a commoner posing as a great man, we learn, and references in the play to his lack of sexual development parallel Hitler's cryptorchidism. Upon his suicide and that of his girl-friend his evil legacy passes to his postwar heirs, in East and West. Special ashes, which the Count says are added to the soup, reflect those from the Nazi ovens, for though the ashes are special, he says, there is nothing special necessary to become special ashes. This image is also closely linked to that in a dream sequence where the cooks threaten to make one of their number into a chimney sweep; that is, they threaten to burn him and send him as smoke up the chimney. (In another scene the Count makes an odd reference to laundry hanging from the ceiling as a symbol for a mass hanging.)

In any case, these cooks—or these governments—continue to pursue each other relentlessly, each one hoping to become the sole heir of evil, each one pre-tending to be white, pretending to provide for its peo-ple, but each one cooking up black catastrophe in-stead.

Other Plays and Poems

After "The Wicked Cooks," Grass's plays and many of his poems become much easier to understand, even as they retain the political, historical symbology of the earlier works. This more transparent tack is an adjunct to his newly evolved direct participation in political matters. Grass begins in 1965 and 1966 to express his political views with increasingly precise clarity in open letters to politicians, in political speeches, essays, and newspaper articles. At the same time the underlying political tenor of his literary works rises closer to the surface, is sharpened, clarified, and enlisted in the cause.

Previous images are now also retroactively linked to such concrete political events as the coming elections. The poem "Gesamtdeutscher März" (Unified German Month of March), for example, mingles references to barbed wire, Marx, Strauss, Ulbricht, and Globke with birds and evil gardeners who stand at attention with their guns. Military scarecrows of NATO and the Warsaw Pact appear, and the whole ends with a blatant political appeal:

> Behold the idyllic scene: Scarecrows
> have marched up to both sides of the Elbe;
> now sparrows are being ideologized . . .
> I advise you to vote for the Social Democratic Party (GG 231).

Grass's deepening commitment to partisan politics and the concomitant sharpening of political images even in his most cryptic lyrical, graphic, and dramatic works is explained and justified in the play *The Plebeians Rehearse the Uprising* (1966). It is based on an earlier essay published in *Akzente* entitled "Vor- und Nachgeschichte der Tragödie des Coriolanus von Livius und Plutarch über Shakespeare bis zu Brecht und mir" (The Pre- and Posthistory of the Tragedy of Coriolanus from Livy and Plutarch via Shakespeare down to Brecht and Me). The play is an apologetic

based on the figure of Bertolt Brecht, a highly respected writer who mixed politics and literature to a
degree previously thought impossible.

Brecht is not mentioned by name in the play, but
is identified for German audiences not only by the title of the preliminary essay but by numerous specific
allusions in the play itself to his life and works.
Building on Brecht's career, Grass takes Brecht one
step further by arguing that one can never be *too* involved in democratic politics: even the great Chief
fails, his lifetime of great work compromised or even
nullified, because on only one occasion, for only a
brief moment, he allows art for art's sake to impede
his participation in political reality.

The setting is East Berlin, the time June 17, 1953.
The Chief and his ensemble rehearse in the confines
of the theater a class-conscious, revolutionary version
of Shakespeare's *Coriolanus*, which involves an uprising of plebeians in ancient Rome. Outside in the
real world, in the here and now, the uprising of real
plebeians begins. The workers send a delegation to
the Chief to ask for his help. If he lends his not in-
considerable intellect, experience, voice, and prestige
to their cause, they feel confident that their peaceful
uprising in the cause of free elections and freer working conditions can succeed.

Without him, however, it will surely fail, for the
workers are like a giant, powerful body (the image of
society as a human body composed of separate, func-
tioning parts is taken from *Coriolanus*) without head,
eyes, or mouth. At the critical moment of *carpe diem,*
however, the great revolutionary writer has fun-

203

damental doubts about the possibility of a German revolution. He contents himself with aesthetic questions, too busy with his art to see the reality outside.

As the uprising fails, crushed by its lack of leadership and ultimately by Soviet armor, the Chief stands alone on the stage. The workers' words echo in his ears, and he realizes he has allowed the historic moment to slip away: "Here stood the mason, born in '22: 'He's writing something there, is that for us?' From there the old socialist said: 'This is our Wednesday, Chief.' What did I say? It doesn't concern me.—The Holy Spirit breathed. I thought it was a draft and cried: who's disturbing me!" (Ts 306). The Chief resigns and goes into retirement, where voices will haunt him the rest of his life.

The Plebeians Rehearse the Uprising is not an attack on Brecht, as some have supposed; it is a defense of Grass and of his political activities, for which he has been so widely criticized. Grass's overriding thesis is that the very purpose of engaged art, the very value of Brecht's genius, lies in his ability to discover truth, to learn to see (like Eddi Amsel), in sharing that vision (like Brauxel), so one can then act, in reality, like Günter Grass. To the extent Brecht slipped into theory, even for a moment, this play implies, he missed an irretrievable historic opportunity to change the world.

Max: A Play, Grass's next and, to date, last drama is, as we have seen, a staged version of the novel *Local Anaesthetic*. The effect on the viewer or the reader is somewhat different for each genre, of course. But because the play and the novel share the same characters, in the same situations, for an understanding of the play what was said above about the novel need not be repeated here.

Similarly, the short plays "Zweiunddreissig Zähne" (Thirty-Two Teeth) (1959) and "Goldmäulchen" (Lil' Goldmouth) (1963) are understandable from the vantage point of *Dog Years* (should they ever be encountered, that is; like the brief curtain-raiser "Rocking Back and Forth" they have not been included in easily accessible editions such as *Theaterspiele*).

The Expository Writings

FOR READERS WHO HAVE DELVED THIS FAR INTO THE
convoluted world of Günter Grass, his relatively
straightforward expository writings—essays,
speeches, open letters, and commentaries—present no
insurmountable problems. Yet the careful reader will
be as much impressed by their wit and fantasy, often
of the highest literary quality, and by what Grass
calls *Doppelbödigkeit*, or that which is stated between the lines, as by their expository clarity on important artistic, historical, and political issues.

A case in point is "Rede von der Gewöhnung"
(Speech about Accommodation, translated "Ben and
Dieter: A Speech to the Israelis") delivered in Tel
Aviv and Jerusalem in early 1967, a few months before the Six-Day War of June 5–10. Appearing on the
surface as a conventional, if somewhat intricate,
admission of German culpability in the Holocaust,
this speech actually far transcends any such perfunc-
tory gesture. It proceeds to examine the problem of
genocide from a wider global and historical perspective. And it ultimately suggests in the most gentle
and subtle way that even Israel itself may be invit-
ing further calamity, a kind of second Holocaust, by

repeating the errors of fascist Germany (precisely because of the trauma inflicted on the Jews *by* fascist
Germany).

For a German to say such things in Israel, of
course, must have required enormous *chutzpa*. But
Grass protected himself by placing at the heart of the
speech a literary narrative, a subtle parable of sorts
in whose correct interpretation lies the very key to
his remarkable political message. For those on whom
the point of this story is lost, Grass had merely made
another digression in a—for them—already rather
disjointed speech.

The story deals, as the English title of the speech
suggests, with Ben and Dieter. The former is a Jewish displaced person or DP, a seventeen-year-old survivor of the concentration camp at Theresienstadt.
The latter is a seventeen-year-old German prisoner
of war or POW, a survivor of the Battle of the Bulge.
Both have been brutalized and dehumanized—reduced to the acronym DP or POW, for example—by
the same evil system, by their experiences under
Nazism. Therefore they join forces in an unlikely
alliance to ridicule and ignore the educational efforts
of one Hermann Mautler, a thirty-year old bespecta-
cled (!) Jewish refugee from Vienna, who had earned
a degree in history at Princeton. He is now a cultural
reeducation officer with the US Army, and is the
very personification of reason and democracy.

But did Hermann Mautler's infinitely patient
reeducation efforts totally fail? Grass hopes not. He
hopes that as mature, forty-year-old Israeli and Ger-

man citizens, respectively, now with family and occupational responsibilities, Ben and Dieter may have become reasonable democrats. The slow-working teachings of Hermann Mautler have certainly affected *him*, at any rate, Grass says, perhaps revealing an autobiographical basis for the story.

And then Grass offers a political variant of the tale that has at least one allegorical leg. Once upon a time there were two wise statesmen, *Ben* Gurion and Konrad Adenauer. But by accommodating themselves to *Realpolitik*, to Adenauer's Nazi associate Hans Globke, for example, were they any more wise and insightful than Ben and Dieter? "Doesn't this story ever want to end? . . . Is this how hi*story* is made? In any case, this is how our hi*story* looks" (ÜS 177), Grass says, broadening his (German) fictional story to global (German and Israeli) factual history.

Having through this tale linked the fate of Germany and the Jews, as he had already done near the end of *Dog Years* and in *From the Diary of a Snail*, it will be recalled, Grass proceeds to review the conventional questions posed by Israelis to Germans about Germany. In this light, however, reflected onto Israel as well, these questions take on more universal meaning: "Have we succeeded in winning the peace? Have we removed the fear of the dark side of our diligence from our neighbors?" (ÜS 178).

Grass ends the speech with an explanation of his peaceful, good intentions and with the following cryptic query addressed to his Israeli hosts: "I only wish to foster the cause of reason. . . . It needs help, *your* help as well. Do you understand me?" (ÜS 179).

As a final note it is necessary to observe that any meaningful reading of the Grass essays requires one to locate a complete text of each. For unknown reasons many of these works have been abridged considerably, apparently at the hands of various editors and translators. The English version of "Ben and Dieter: A Speech to the Israelis," for example, as published in *Speak Out!* is missing a full seven pages between the first and second paragraphs. Without this important material it is impossible to see Grass's entire subtle strategy.

Nor are the German collections themselves free from such omissions. As originally published in the *Süddeutsche Zeitung* (January 12-13, 1974), for example, Grass's very significant and revealing article "Rückblick auf die Blechtrommel—oder: Der Autor als fragwürdiger Zeuge" ("The Tin Drum in Retrospect or The Author as Dubious Witness") was 112 column inches long. When it appeared in *Aufsätze zur Literatur* (the version on which the English translation is also based), 48 percent of the text, comprising some of the most significant information, had been omitted.

BIBLIOGRAPHY

Works by Günter Grass

Die Vorzüge der Windhühner (The Advantages of Wind Chickens). Neuwied: Luchterhand, 1956. Portions in *Selected Poems,* trans. Michael Hamburger and Christopher Middleton; London: Secker & Warburg, 1966; and *In the Egg and Other Poems,* trans. Michael Hamburger and Christopher Middleton; New York: Harcourt Brace, 1977.

Hochwasser. (Premiered 1957 in Frankfurt.) Frankfurt: Suhrkamp, 1963. ["Flood." Trans. Ralph Manheim. *Four Plays.* New York: Harcourt Brace, 1967. 1–74.]

Onkel, Onkel. (Premiered 1958 in Cologne.) Rev. ed. Berlin: Wagenbach, 1965. ["Mister, Mister." Trans. Ralph Manheim. *Four Plays.* New York: Harcourt Brace, 1967. 75–164.]

"Noch zehn Minuten bis Buffalo." (Premiered 1959 in Bochum.) *Akzente* 5 (1958): 5–17. ["Only Ten Minutes to Buffalo." Trans. Ralph Manheim. *Four Plays.* New York: Harcourt Brace, 1967. 165–88.]

Die Blechtrommel. Neuwied: Luchterhand, 1959. [*The Tin Drum.* Trans. Ralph Manheim. New York: Harcourt Brace, 1961.]

Gleisdreieck (Three-rail Junction). Neuwied: Luchterhand, 1960. Portions in *Selected Poems,* trans. Michael Hamburger and Christopher Middleton; London: Secker & Warburg, 1966; and *In the Egg and Other Poems,* trans. Michael Hamburger and Christopher Middleton; New York: Harcourt Brace, 1977.

Katz und Maus. Neuwied: Luchterhand, 1961. [*Cat and Mouse*. Trans. Ralph Manheim. New York: Harcourt Brace, 1963.]

Die bösen Köche. (Premiered 1961 in Berlin.) Berlin: Kiepenheuer, 1961. ["The Wicked Cooks." Trans. A. Leslie Willson. *Four Plays*. New York: Harcourt Brace, 1967. 189–289.]

Hundejahre. Neuwied: Luchterhand, 1963. [*Dog Years*. Trans. Ralph Manheim. New York: Harcourt Brace, 1965.]

Die Plebejer proben den Aufstand. (Premiered 1966 in Berlin.) Neuwied: Luchterhand, 1966. [*The Plebeians Rehearse the Uprising*. Trans. Ralph Manheim. New York: Harcourt Brace, 1966.]

Ausgefragt (Thoroughly Interrogated). Neuwied: Luchterhand, 1967. Portions in *New Poems,* trans. Michael Hamburger; New York: Harcourt Brace, 1968; and *In the Egg and Other Poems,* trans. Michael Hamburger and Christopher Middleton; New York: Harcourt Brace, 1977.

Über das Selbstverständliche: Reden, Aufsätze, offene Briefe, Kommentare (On the Self-evident: Speeches, Essays, Open Letters, Commentaries). Neuwied: Luchterhand, 1968. Portions in *Speak Out! Speeches, Open Letters, Commentaries*. Trans. Ralph Manheim et al. New York: Harcourt Brace, 1969.

Briefe über die Grenze: Versuch eines Ost-West Dialogs (Letters Across the Border: An Attempt at an East-West Dialogue). Hamburg: Wegner, 1968.

Davor. (Premiered 1969 in Berlin.) Berlin: Kiepenheuer, 1969. [*Max: A Play*. Trans. A. Leslie Willson and Ralph Manheim. New York: Harcourt Brace, 1972.]

örtlich betäubt. Neuwied: Luchterhand, 1969. [*Local Anaesthetic*. Trans. Ralph Manheim. New York: Harcourt Brace, 1970.]

Theaterspiele (Plays). Neuwied: Luchterhand, 1970.

Gesammelte Gedichte (Collected Poems). Neuwied: Luchterhand, 1971.

Aus dem Tagebuch einer Schnecke. Neuwied: Luchterhand, 1972. [*From the Diary of a Snail*. Trans. Ralph Manheim. New York: Harcourt Brace, 1973.]

Mariazuehren. Munich: Bruckmann, 1973. [*Inmarypraise*. Trans. Christopher Middleton. New York: Harcourt Brace, 1973.]

Liebe geprüft. Bremen: Schünemann, 1974. [*Love Tested*. Trans. Michael Hamburger. New York: Harcourt Brace, 1975.]

Der Bürger und seine Stimme: Reden, Aufsätze, Kommentare (The Citizen and His Voice: Speeches, Essays, Commentaries). Neuwied: Luchterhand, 1974. Portions in *On Writing and Politics 1967–1983* Trans. Ralph Manheim. New York: Harcourt Brace, 1985.

Der Butt. Neuwied: Luchterhand, 1977. [*The Flounder*. Trans. Ralph Manheim. New York: Harcourt Brace, 1978.]

Denkzettel: Politische Reden und Aufsätze 1965–1976 (Memoranda: Political Speeches and Essays 1965–1976). Neuwied: Luchterhand, 1978. Portions in *On Writing and Politics 1967–1983,* Trans. Ralph Manheim. New York: Harcourt Brace, 1985.

Das Treffen in Telgte. Neuwied: Luchterhand, 1979. [*The Meeting at Telgte*. Trans. Ralph Manheim. New York: Harcourt Brace, 1981.]

Kopfgeburten oder Die Deutschen sterben aus. Neuwied: Luchterhand, 1980. [*Headbirths or The Germans Are Dying Out*. Trans. Ralph Manheim. New York: Harcourt Brace, 1982.]

Aufsätze zur Literatur (Essays on Literature). Neuwied: Luchterhand, 1980. Portions in *On Writing and Politics 1967–1983*. Trans. Ralph Manheim. New York: Harcourt Brace, 1985.

Zeichnen und Schreiben, Band I: Zeichnungen und Texte 1954–1977. Neuwied: Luchterhand, 1982. [*Drawings & Words Nineteen Fifty-Four to Nineteen Seventy-Seven*. Trans. Walter Arndt and Michael Hamburger. New York: Harcourt Brace, 1982.]

Ach Butt, dein Märchen geht böse aus (Alas, Flounder, Your Fairy Tale Has an Unhappy Ending). Neuwied: Luchterhand, 1983.

Widerstand lernen: Politische Gegenreden 1980–1983 (Learn to Resist: Political Rebuttals 1980–1983). Neuwied: Luchterhand, 1984. Portions in *On Writing and Politics 1967–1983*. Trans. Ralph Manheim. New York: Harcourt Brace, 1985.

Zeichnen und Schreiben, Band II: Radierungen und Texte 1972–1982. Neuwied: Luchterhand, 1984. [*Etchings & Words Nineteen Seventy-Two to Nineteen Eighty-Two*. Trans. Michael Hamburger et al. New York: Harcourt Brace, 1985.]

Die Rättin. Neuwied: Luchterhand, 1986. [*The Rat*. Trans. Ralph Manheim. New York: Harcourt Brace, 1987.]

In Kupfer, auf Stein (In Copper, On Stone). Göttingen: Steidl, 1986.

Critical Works

Bibliographies

Everett, George A. *A Select Bibliography of Günter Grass (From 1956 to 1973)*. New York: Burt Franklin, 1974.

Görtz, Franz Josef. "Kommentierte Auswahlbibliographie (Annotated Select Bibliography)." *Text+Kritik, Heft 1/1a, Günter Grass*. Ed. Heinz Ludwig Arnold. Munich: Edition Text+Kritik, [5]1978. 175–99.

O'Neill, Patrick. *Günter Grass: A Bibliography 1955–1975*. Toronto: University of Toronto Press, 1976.

Woods, Jean M. "Günter Grass Bibliography." *West Coast Review* 5.3 (1971): 52–56, and 6.1 (1971): 31–40.

Books

Arnold, Heinz Ludwig, and Görtz, Franz Josef, eds. *Günter Grass: Dokumente zur politischen Wirkung*. Munich: Edition Text + Kritik, 1971. An invaluable collection of newspaper clippings, correspondence, and other documentation of Grass's stormy political career; and of such controversial matters as the Bremen Literary Prize, legal action against Kurt Ziesel (who accused Grass of pornography), the Kipphardt affair, and Grass's battles with the Springer press.

Brode, Hanspeter. *Günter Grass*. Munich: Beck, 1979. Perhaps the best short introduction to Grass in German.

———. *Die Zeitgeschichte im erzählenden Werk von Günter Grass*. Frankfurt: Lang, 1977. Treats the Danzig trilogy and *Local Anaesthetic* as history, suggesting they belong alongside such other fictive histories of the Third Reich as Uwe Johnson's *Jahrestage* and Siegfried Lenz's *Deutschstunde*. Ends with a methodological excursus on reception theory.

Cunliffe, W. Gordon. *Günter Grass*. New York: Twayne, 1969. A useful and balanced introduction to Grass in English, albeit only through the Danzig trilogy and *The Plebeians Rehearse the Uprising*.

Diller, Edward. *A Mythic Journey: Günter Grass's "Tin Drum."* Lexington: The University Press of Kentucky, 1974. An interesting mythic study of the Great Mother figure, the black cook/white nurse dichotomy, and the chthonic descent to the underworld, which has an Achilles' heel: it fails to comprehend that these mythic overtones cannot simply be taken at face value, since they are largely a function of Oskar's megalomanic delusions and of his posturing. Diller also takes name symbolism decidedly too far, as when he tries to show that the Polish name Bronski is derived from German *Brunnen* (fountain, source, spring).

Durzak, Manfred, ed. *Interpretationen zu Günter Grass. Geschichte auf dem poetischen Prüfstand*. Stuttgart: Klett, 1985. A collection of ten articles, a foreword, and an interview, dealing with a broad spectrum of Grass's works up to *Headbirths*. Includes a useful annotated bibliography.

Geissler, Rolf, ed. *Günter Grass. Ein Materialienbuch*. Neuwied: Luchterhand, 1976. A collection of seven essays about Grass and his works as well as three by Grass himself, together with a useful bibliography.

Görtz, Franz Josef, ed. *"Die Blechtrommel" Attraktion und Ärgernis*. Neuwied: Luchterhand, 1984. A collection of critical reactions to *The Tin Drum* which document its polarized reception.

———, ed. *Günter Grass: Auskunft für Leser*. Neuwied: Luchterhand, 1984. A valuable collection of twenty-three essays, interviews, and other documents by Grass and others about many aspects of Grass's life and works, including an excellent bibliography.

Hayman, Ronald. *Günter Grass*. London: Methuen, 1985. A 65-page book which despite its brevity presents a useful view of themes in Grass, arranged under such headings as puppets and ballerinas, drums and eels, cats and dogs, teeth and snails.

Jurgensen, Manfred, ed. *Grass. Kritik—Thesen—Analysen*. Bern: Francke, 1973. Thirteen essays on Grass, each chosen to represent one of a wide variety of schools of thought.

———. *Über Günter Grass*. Bern: Francke, 1974. An examination in the main of the aesthetics of the poems and dramas, with brief references to some prose works,

215

arguing that Grass's thought is at bottom plastic and object oriented, which allows it to be translated productively into so many different media.

Krumme, Detlef. *Günter Grass Die Blechtrommel*. Munich: Hanser, 1986. A useful introductory commentary on *The Tin Drum* which briefly illuminates many different facets of the novel from inception to reception. It includes a discussion of the so-called *Urtrommel*, a typescript of an early version of the novel discovered in Paris by John Reddick.

Lawson, Richard H. *Günter Grass*. New York: Ungar, 1985. This short and readable book is a good first introduction in English to the life of Günter Grass and to the plots and characters of his works through *Headbirths*. Most attempts at interpretation are, however, more sketched in than fleshed out.

Leonard, Irène. *Günter Grass*. New York: Barnes and Noble, 1974. A useful short book in English which briefly discusses the Danzig trilogy and then discourses on the writer as political activist and vice versa; on imagery, structure, and style, as well as on the critical reception of Grass's works.

Loschütz, Gert, ed. *Von Buch zu Buch—Günter Grass in der Kritik. Eine Dokumentation*. Neuwied: Luchterhand, 1968. Review of Grass's books in contemporary newspapers, including excerpts from some foreign papers, are here collected in one useful volume.

Mason, Ann L. *The Skeptical Muse: A Study of Günter Grass' Conception of the Artist*. Bern: Lang, 1974. An insightful examination (through *Local Anaesthetic*) of Grass's attempts to create meaningful works of art in the German language and in a symbolical, mythical cosmology, both of which had been grossly prostituted by Nazism. His use of artist-protagonists such as Oskar and Eddi is explained, as are the aesthetic implications of his political involvement.

Mews, Siegfried, ed. *"The Fisherman and His Wife": Günter Grass's "The Flounder" in Critical Perspective*. New York: AMS Press, 1983. Thirteen essays on as many aspects of *The Flounder*, valuable also for the appendixes, which include a structural diagram of the months, places, periods, cooks, and narrators of the novel.

Miles, Keith. *Günter Grass*. New York: Barnes and Noble, 1975. A good medium-sized study in English of Grass through *From the Diary of a Snail*, marred only by an occasional lengthy digression and by an odd conclusion attempted in the style of Oskar Matzerath.

Neuhaus, Volker. *Günter Grass*. Stuttgart: Metzler, 1979. An excellent short treatise on Grass through *The Meeting in Telgte*, including a short diagram of *The Flounder* and a bibliography.

————. *Günter Grass Die Blechtrommel*. Munich: Oldenbourg, 1982. An expansion of the chapter on *The Tin Drum* in Neuhaus's *Günter Grass*, this small book is also useful for its discussion of the film version of the novel.

O'Neill, Patrick, ed. *Critical Essays on Günter Grass*. Boston: Hall, 1987. A collection of twenty-one excellent reviews and essays previously published in periodicals, with two original essays by the editor, including one on *The Rat*.

Pickar, Gertrude Bauer, ed. *Adventures of a Flounder: Critical Essays on Günter Grass' "Der Butt."* Munich: Fink, 1982. Ten views of *The Flounder,* ranging from a fiercely polemical feminist response to a subtle demonstration of its structural sophistication.

Reddick, John. *The "Danzig Trilogy" of Günter Grass*. New York: Harcourt Brace, 1975. An informative, stimulating, and at the same time somewhat disappointing book by an author who has interviewed and corresponded with Grass very often, and who sees the "trees" of his work as well as any other, yet who often misses the "forest" in which they stand. Some of his objections—to the "last 2/

5" of *Dog Years*, for example—seem unfounded and odd, and the book often seems otherwise disjointed.

Tank, Kurt Lothar. *Günter Grass*. New York: Ungar, 1969. A translation of the German edition of 1965, this book is an easy, if somewhat informal and cursory, work on Grass's life, his early poems and plays, and the Danzig trilogy.

Thomas, Noel. *The Narrative Works of Günter Grass: A Critical Interpretation*. Amsterdam: Benjamins, 1982. A dissertation useful for its attention to details in the texts, but somewhat flawed by its hesitancy to base an interpretive argument on them.

Vormweg, Heinrich. *Günter Grass, mit Selbstzeugnissen und Bilddokumenten*. Reinbek: Rowohlt, 1986. A very valuable small book in the Rowohlt *Bildmonographien* series by a knowledgeable and sensitive contemporary and confidant of Grass who had access to many previously unpublished photos and other documentary material.

Wieser, Theodor, ed. *Günter Grass. Porträt und Poesie*. Neuwied: Luchterhand, 1968. A substantial essay by the editor about Grass's poetry is followed by selected poems and short prose pieces of Günter Grass himself, interspersed with twenty-seven reproductions of photographs of Grass and his family and of Grass's graphic work.

Willson, A. Leslie, ed. *A Günter Grass Symposium*. Austin: University of Texas Press, 1971. Six excellent essays on aspects of the poetry, plays, and prose fiction.

Articles

Because of the great number of articles about Grass, and because many of the best of them have been included in collections listed above, for additional references the reader is advised to consult the bibliographies of Everett, Görtz, O'Neill, and Woods.

Interviews

Arnold, Heinz Ludwig. "Gespräche mit Günter Grass."
Text + Kritik, Heft 1/1a, Günter Grass. Ed. Heinz Ludwig
Arnold. Munich: Edition Text + Kritik, [5]1978. 1–39.

———. "Antrag auf Scheidung von meinen Kritikern." *Als
Schriftsteller leben*. Ed. Heinz Ludwig Arnold. Reinbek:
Rowohlt, 1979. 140–55.

Grass, Günter. *Atelier des métamorphoses, entretiens avec
Nicole Casanova*. Paris: Belfond, 1979.

Rudolph, Ekkehart. "Günter Grass." *Aussage zur Person*.
Ed. Ekkehart Rudolph. Tübingen: Erdmann, 1977. 83–
100.

Van D'Elden, Karl H. "Günter Grass." *West German Poets
on Society and Politics*. Ed. Karl H. Van D'Elden. De-
troit: Wayne State University Press, 1979. 162–79.

Archive

The Günter Grass Archive is located at the Deutsches
Literaturarchiv, Postfach 57, D-7142 Marbach A.N.,
Federal Republic of Germany.

INDEX

241